A Collegial Bishop Revisited

Deddens Kerkrecht Serie / Deddens Series in Church Polity - 4

Edited by Leon van den Broeke (Amsterdam / Kampen)
in cooperation with
Klaas-Willem de Jong (Amsterdam / Groningen)
Pieter T. Pel (Hattem)
Herman J. Selderhuis (Apeldoorn)
Johannes Smit (Potchefstroom)
Kathy Smith (Grand Rapids)

Vol. 1: Leon van den Broeke (red.) *De collectioneur: De kerkrechtelijke nalatenschap van D. Deddens* (2018)
Vol. 3: Leon van den Broeke en Hans Schaeffer (red.) *Geest of Recht? Kerkrecht tussen ideaal en werkelijkheid*

LEON VAN DEN BROEKE AND ALLAN J. JANSSEN (EDS.)

A Collegial Bishop Revisited

Classis and Presbytery at Issue

Summum

© 2020 Summum Academic Publications - Kampen
www.summumacademic.com

Cover design: Brainstorm
Interior design: Gewoon Geertje

ISBN 9789492701145
ISSN 2590-0404

All rights reserved.

Content

List of abbreviations   7

In memoriam Allan Jay Janssen (1948-2020)
    Leon van den Broeke   9

Preface   15
    René de Reuver

Introduction   19
    Leon van den Broeke

Who Says? The Authority of the Classis/Presbytery in a Reformed Church   27
    Allan J. Janssen

For What Reason is the Classis on Earth? The Classis as a Buffer between Ecclesial Individualism and Regional Catholicity in the Context of Globalization, Regionalism and Glocalization   37
    Leon van den Broeke

Half a Bishop: A Critical Outline of the So-called *Classispredikant* in the Protestant Church in the Netherlands   55
    Klaas-Willem de Jong

Balancing Tensions and Encouraging Health: The Classis Renewal Movement in the Christian Reformed Church in North America   73
    Kathleen S. Smith

Classis in the Evangelical Church of Czech Brethren   85
    Adam Csukás

How Polity Dies: Form without Substance in the Presbyterian Church (U.S.A.)   103
    Joseph D. Small

Presbytery as the Engine of the Church   119
    JOHN P. CHALMERS

Afterword   135
    ALLAN J. JANSSEN

The authors   139

Index   141

List of abbreviations

BEM	Baptist, Eucharist and Ministry-report
CRCNA	Christian Reformed Church in North America
DCO	Dort Church Order
ECCB	Evangelical Church of Czech Brethren
PCN	Protestant Church in the Netherlands (*Protestantse Kerk in Nederland*)
PCUSA	Presbyterian Church United Stated of America
RCA	Reformed Church in America
URC	United Reformed Church

Photographer Gerrit van Dijk. Picture included with permission of the Reformatorisch Dagblad

In memoriam Allan Jay Janssen (1948-2020)

Leon van den Broeke

On Friday 20 March 2020 Al and I finished the manuscript of this book and sent it to the publisher. The next day we continued exchanging e-mails, among others about the COVID19-virus. On Al's birthday, Tuesday 31 March, I received word from his successor, Matthew van Maastricht, that Al was in hospital. His situation did not look good. The news came as a shock. Three days later (American time) the real shock came: Al had died.

It is hard to imagine that Allan Jay Janssen has gone, especially for Colleen, his wife, his children and grandchildren, the community of the New Brunswick Theological Seminary and the Reformed Church in America (RCA), but also for the wider ecclesial and theological community on both sides of the ocean. Although he was not a networker *pur sang*, Al had a large ecclesial and academic network. It was his passion for the church, the creeds and confessions, polity and the theology of the offices which connected him with others around the globe. To him the church was *creatura verbi*, creation by the Word of God and a foretaste of God's Kingdom. He spoke highly of the church without idealizing it, as the oldest son of a pastor he understood that. At the same time, he was down-to-earth enough to observe the attitude of office-bearers, consistories or synods who made, in his mind, the wrong decisions and/or decisions in the wrong way. He could be annoyed by this and at the same talk about it in a hilarious way with a big smile on his face. Seeing this did not stop him from respecting the church of his childhood and, in the past half-century, in which he operated as a theologian. In all of this, he expressed his passion for theology and the church.

Al studied at Central College in Pella, Iowa and at the so-called Bi-Level Multi-Site Programme of the RCA of the Western Theological Seminary in Holland, Michigan and the New Brunswick Theological Seminary. He served the congregations in Port Ewen, New York; The First Reformed Church of Bethlehem in Selkirk, New York; the Community Church in Glen Rock, New Jersey. From 1999 he taught at New Brunswick

Theological Seminary, as from 2006 he became Affiliate Professor, in 2012 General Synod Professor and in 2018 Emeritus Professor.

Al was keen on ecclesial developments in the Netherlands and the Dutch theology. On a daily basis he read and watched the Dutch news as well as the church news. In addition to his American colleagues, he maintained contacts with many Dutch theologians and others around the globe. He always tried to combine things on trips and looked forward to the highlights in his professional life: the bi-annual conferences of the International Reformed Theological Institute and the Summer School of the New Brunswick Theological Seminary at the Protestantse Theologische Universiteit/Vrije Universiteit Amsterdam. The Vrije Universiteit was the place where, in June 2005, he defended his doctoral research about the Netherlands Reformed theologian Arnold A. van Ruler (1908-1970): *Kingdom, Office, and Church: A Study of A.A. van Ruler's Doctrine of Ecclesiastical Office*. The Dutch theologian Bram van de Beek and the South African theologian Christo Lombard were his supervisors. In 2000 he had already published his *Constitutional Theology: Notes on the Book of Church Order of the Reformed Church in America*. In 2019 a second (revised) edition saw the light.

As a pastor Al remained a professor, and as a professor he was a pastor. He could not separate these roles. They belonged together, because the theological nature of the church was too important for him. The church was according to him *creatura verbi*, a creation of the Word of God. Therefore, he loved to teach not only Church Polity, but also Credo.

Since the day we met, on Tuesday 10 April 2007 at New Brunswick Theological Seminary, we never stopped talking about *credo*, church, ecclesiology, the theology of the offices, sacramentology, church polity, and about the classis. In fact, for me, my discussion with him had already started in 2000 when I ordered his book *Gathered at Albany: A History of Classis*. It was a delight to study it and to use it for my doctoral dissertation. Nevertheless, I had to wait seven years before we could meet. From that day, we never stopped talking and exchanging e-mails, organizing conferences and meeting each other in American, Dutch and South African universities, seminaries, church buildings, restaurants and our homes.

On 1 April 2008 we organized our first conference on the middle assembly and judicatory level: the classis and the presbytery. The conference took place at the New Brunswick Theological Seminary. Two years later the conference proceedings were released: *A Collegial Bishop: The Classis and Presbytery at Issue*, in the *Historical Series of the Reformed Church in America*. Al and I were the editors. Since then, we saw rapidly growing developments and ecclesial and societal changes for the classis and the presbytery, and in general for the presbyteral-synodical system of church governance. We discussed their nature, the (im)possibility of a non-geographic classis in the RCA. Our conversations resulted in my article in the *Journal of Reformed Theology*: "Non-Geographic Classis: Reformed Geography".[1] Developments increased, both in North America and in the Netherlands, and not only these, but other parts of the globe, including the Global South.

It gave rise to the thought of another conference and a second book on the classis and the presbytery. Al preferred to have the conference in the Netherlands this time, and we held this conference on 22 and 23 Mary 2018. Although he was a frequent guest in the Netherlands and especially at the Vrije Universiteit Amsterdam it was his first time to visit and work at the Theologische Universiteit Kampen. When he arrived he gave me a copy of his book, *Confessing the Faith Today: A Fresh Look at the Belgic Confession*. It is an expression of his theology and the result of many years teaching *Credo* (in Dutch: *Symboliek*). Due to his physical condition he arrived in bad shape. I was worried and kept an extra eye on him during that time. He seemed to enjoy dinner, and also the wine, and he recovered a bit. He so much enjoyed the conference, the conversations, the food and the fellowship. Although he recovered a bit during the conference, he had a bad flight back home due to his illness.

A year later he was back at the Vrije Universiteit for the IRTI-conference and a meeting with view to the progress of the doctoral research of his successor, Matthew van Maastricht. He expected much of Matthew and was happy to have him as his successor. As an aside, I am grateful that Matthew was willing to help me with an extra grammar check of the book print! Al enjoyed the meeting we had as supervisors (including supervisor professor George Harinck) of Van Maastricht's doctoral project. Afterwards Al also enjoyed a good dinner, nice wine, a profound ecclesial and theological conversation and stories full of humor. Al was in much better shape, both physically and mentally. During that Summer we continued our work on the conference proceedings. He wrote an epilogue which most probably was, if not his last, one of his last articles.

As said before, Al and I had already sent the manuscript to the publisher. Nevertheless, the publisher understood my wish when I shared the news that Al had died and gave me the opportunity to include words

---

1 Van den Broeke, "Non-Geographic Classis?".

of remembrance and a picture of Al which are included in the book.[2] The picture is taken by Gerrit van Dijk, journalist/photographer of the Dutch newspaper *Reformatorisch Dagblad*. Al read that newspaper daily. At the conference Van Dijk interviewed Al about his passion for the Dutch theologian A.A. van Ruler.[3] Al was surprised about this interest and the article and his picture in the newspaper. The *Reformatorisch Dagblad* gave permission to include this picture in the book for which I am very grateful.

It its hard that Al has died and that he cannot see the book again. On the website of the RCA there is this impressive, accurate and well-written quote about Al: "He lived as a true servant of the church, and died tragically isolated from family and friends, but in the friendship of Christ."[4]

We try to continue our lives with the same faith, the same respect for the church, and the same passion for theology and church polity as Al had, and with the same friendship of Christ. At the end of his book *Confessing the Faith Today* Al concluded:

We give witness that we have heard God speak, God's Word in Scripture (…). Those Scriptures are filled with promise, promise for the future. The promise is for a broken world, that a creation that has been besmirched will be purified. God's promises have been "sealed" in the sacraments (…). For the individual person, the promise is of resurrection and of judgment that will make all things well. The promise is of a community and a communion where "the home of God is among mortals. He will dwell with them as their God; they will be his peoples, and God himself will be with them; he will wipe away every tear from their eyes. Death will be no more; mourning and crying and pain will be no more, for the first things have passed away" (Rev 21:3,4). We can witness that the promise has been provisionally and really fulfilled in Christ. The Spirit wakens hope within us and within our community. On that basis we look forward with hope.[5]

April 2020

---

2 See also another *in memoriam* (in Dutch) at: accessed 22 April 2020, http://www.kerkrecht.nl/content/allan-j-janssen-1948–2020
3 Accessed 22 April 2020, https://www.rd.nl/kerk-religie/subscription-required-7.133?aId =1.1492119
4 Accessed 22 April 2020, https://www.rca.org/news/remembering-allan-janssen
5 Janssen, *Confessing the Faith Today*, 150.

Bibliography

Janssen, Allan J. *Confessing the Faith Today: A Fresh Look at the Belgic Confession*. Eugene OR: WIPF & Stock, 2016.

Janssen, Allan J. and Leon van den Broeke, eds. *A Collegial Bishop: Classis and Presbytery at Issue*. Grand Rapids MI: Wm. B. Eerdmans, 2010 (*The Historical Series in the Reformed Church in America* 66).

Janssen, Allan J. *Kingdom, Office, and Church: A Study of A.A. van Ruler's Doctrine of Ecclesiastical Office*. diss. VU Amsterdam. Grand Rapids MI: Wm. B. Eerdmans, 2006 (*The Historical Series of the Reformed Church in America* 53).

Janssen, Allan J. *Constitutional Theology: Notes on the Book of Church Order of the Reformed Church in America*. 2nd ed. Grand Rapids MI: Wm. B. Eerdmans, 2019 (*The Historical Series of the Reformed Church in America* 100).

Janssen, Allan J. *Constitutional Theology: Notes on the Book of Church Order of the Reformed Church in America*. Grand Rapids MI, 2000 (*The Historical Series of the Reformed Church in America* 33).

Janssen, Allan J. *Gathered at Albany: A History of Classis*. Grand Rapids MI: Wm. B. Eerdmans, 1995 (*The Historical Series of the Reformed Church in America* 25).

Van den Broeke, Leon. "Non-Geographic Classis? Reformed Geography," *Journal of Reformed Theology* (2013) n°. 7/1, 51–68.

Digital sources
http://www.kerkrecht.nl/content/allan-j-janssen-1948-2020.

https://www.rca.org/news/remembering-allan-janssen

https://www.rd.nl/kerk-religie/subscription-required-7.133?aId=1.1492119

Preface

René de Reuver

Reorientation
In 2018 the Protestant Church in the Netherlands (PCN) completed a rather fundamental reorganization of the church structure. The eleven newly formed classes have appointed a new kind of protestant bishop, the so called: classis minister (in Dutch: *classispredikant*). The process of reorganization did not begin as a process of restructuring, but as a process of reorientation. A couple of years ago the General Synod of the PCN adopted a paper in which a vision on the church was developed. It started with a statement on the origins of the church: Its basic principle is that the church is a Jesus movement that has its beginnings in the resurrection of Jesus Christ. Its foundation is the Triune God, the life he gives us, the reconciliation and the comfort that he promises us. We live from grace. Not what we believe, have thought of or achieved is the decisive factor; the real issue is what, as an absolute surprise, is presented to us by Jesus.[1]

Why should we revisit and rethink the church? Primarily because the church is also an organization with a structure, rules and regulations. That is the way the church operates and works in this world. It is an orderly and well-arranged institution, which aims at the communion with the living Lord, Jesus Christ. However, it seems as if this core picture of the church is becoming blurred.

The church as a burden?
Not so long ago the church belonged to society and revolved around the local congregation, the church council and the minister, the buildings, the lectionary and the financial resources. This is no longer a matter of course. And, in addition, many churches in our secular society have become smaller. Fewer people have to do all the tasks. Many matters have to be taken care of, an ever-decreasing number of volunteers has to

---

[1] Cf. *De Hartslag van het leven: Visie op het leven en werken van de Protestantse Kerk in Nederland* (Utrecht/Zoetermeer: Protestantse Kerk in Nederland/Boekencentrum, z.j.), 14; accessed 7 February 2020, http://www.protestantsekerk.nl.

perform an ever increasing number of tasks. The schedules become overcrowded with items and joy disappears. The church becomes a burden rather than a source of joy.

However, we cannot live without rules and regulations. They are in fact the rules by which we have to play the game. The fact is that we live in a dramatically changed society in which the church and other institutions are not only losing members, but are also seen as becoming irrelevant in society. Serving in an office in the church often becomes a burden. First because of the many necessary meetings and second because it becomes difficult to find members of the congregation who are willing to serve as an elder or as a deacon.

As a presbyterial-synodical church, we also have to cope with the fact that the task of governing in the church is often accumulated. When you are member of the local church board, it is possible that you will become a delegate to the classis. And as a delegate to the classis you might be elected as a delegate to the General Synod. This all takes a lot of time and isn't always inspiring. Many meetings are all about making decisions on the governance of the church.

'Back to basics'
As I noted above, a few years ago the General Synod decided to become cognizant of this situation and to ask: why are we doing all these things? Why are we members of the church? What is it all about? Is it not all about the gospel of Jesus Christ, about his love and compassion, about his death and his resurrection? Is that not the ground under our feet, the horizon before us and the power of our lives? If that is the case, why are we struggling to maintain an institution that is top-heavy?

So, a couple of years ago the General Synod decided to 'go back to basics'. What does this mean? First, that we have to cut all kinds of regulations in the church order. The responsibility of the congregation in her own context has to be stressed. Not everything the congregation does and plans has to be regulated. The Synod decided that local congregations should get all possible opportunities to really go back to basics. Less time should be given to maintaining the structure of the institution. Of course the church is also an institution that has to be managed and governed. But the 'technical' matters of governance of the church have to be transferred to a larger structure that will have professional support. An inspiring *episkopē* will receive face and form in the classes through appointed classis ministers. All this is what we call 'Church 2025'.

The classis: The fundamental assembly
So in the new structure, the classis as such will not disappear. On the contrary, the newly formed larger classes with the eleven classis ministers can be seen as the engine for the development of the regional church. The character of the classis, as a platform for the congregations in a certain area, as a *conventus ecclesiarum*, will not change. In the classis all the offices are represented. Decisions are made by the collectivity of the offices. This is the strength of the Reformed way of being a church. The church lives from the bottom up. Decisions are made not parachuted from the sky, hierarchically, but arise from the deliberation of the offices.

In this perspective, the classis can be called the fundamental assembly of the church. The classis is not the sum of all the individual congregations only. It is more than that. It is an ecclesiastical body on its own. In the Reformed perspective, the classis fulfills one of the episcopal functions, that of overseer. This aspect is primarily a pastoral aspect. Congregations are called and challenged to be a pastor for each other. This aspect is strongly connected with the aspect of unity. Like the bishop in the Roman Catholic Church, the classis embodies the unity of the church and is personified in the figure of the classis minister. The congregations with all their different colors, are not individual entities that have their own existence. They belong to each other as the members of one body. They look after each other (visitation), they are called to correct each other (discipline), and together (as a unity) they are responsible for the life and the work of the church in their region.

New structure
The process of reorientation of the church ('back to basics') also leads to a lighter structure that should help the local congregations to live the Gospel of Jesus Christ, and to experience the church as a communion of hope. What does this practically mean for the actual situation of the church? Until 1 May 2018, the PCN consisted of 74 classical bodies. Each classis chooses one member as a delegate to the General Synod. This means that the General Synod consisted of 74 members. Now however, this number has been reduced to 11 classical bodies. Each classis is supported by a so-called classis minister. He or she is responsible for the support of the life and the work of the local congregations and for inspiring and supporting the local pastors. He or she has some elements of a bishop, but we don't call him or her a bishop. The governance of the church in a presbyterial-synodical system is always and will always be delegated to a body consisting of several offices. In the new structure the

classis minister cannot make fundamental decisions on his or her own. There is always the element of presbyterial governance. The newly shaped classis is not an episcopal body. It is rather a platform where the congregations will meet and where they will be responsible for building each other up in faith, in hope, in love.

All of this this means that the newly formed classis still bears the elements and aspects that the sixteenth-century Protestant Reformation has found valuable for the life and work of the church. It combines some of the episcopal elements with that, of what can be called the cornerstone of the Reformed approach to the office, the office of the elder. The elder as the embodiment of the bottom up approach in Reformed ecclesiology. Ecclesiologically said: presbyterial-synodical and not episcopal.

By the way: the former 74 classes will not vanish. They can be transformed into what we call a 'ring': a regional assembly consisting of a group of congregations in a certain area. The meeting within this assembly will not focus on the governance of the church, but it will be a platform of sharing and meeting. Congregations can share the stumbling blocks they experience, the solutions they have found, share knowledge and share inspiration.

Joy
It is hoped that this newly shaped system will lead in the end to discussions and decisions in the General Synod, which really will arise from the bottom of the church: the local congregations, their needs, their struggle and their challenges. And above all that the eleven newly formed classes with the classis ministers will inspire the local churches to be church in their context, with joy, hope and compassion. May this book find its way into the denominations worldwide that have classes or presbyteries. That it may inspire and motivate the boards and the members of such bodies, the denominations in general and help the theological reflection to re-find old ways and to find new ways that classes and presbyteries worldwide in whatever societal, political and ecclesial context are places of joy, hope and compassion.

Utrecht, Christmas 2019

Introduction

Leon van den Broeke

Motivation

"The classis is more under pressure than I thought." On 22-23 May 2018 one of the participants made this statement at the international conference on the classis and the presbytery at the Theologische Universiteit Kampen in the Netherlands. Ten years earlier, on 1 April 2008, my co-editor and colleague Allan J. Janssen and I organized the previous international conference on the classis and the presbytery at the New Brunswick Theological Seminary in the United States of America. By that time there was already an experience of communalities, because of what was considered as the classis and the presbytery under pressure. This process has continued, and even increased. Not only because of the increasing depreciation of the classis and the presbytery, but also because of the depreciation and decreasing knowledge among office-bearers of church polity in general and the misunderstanding of what it is, ought to be and the consequences for all the general assemblies, like the classis and the presbytery. Reformed and Presbyterian denominations around the globe struggle with church polity, the understanding and the application of their books of church order. They fool around with structure, classis and presbytery.

The classis is the community of neighboring local churches, as stated by the General Synod of Emden of 1571 in Article 7 of its Acts.[1] Every consistory delegates office-bearers to the classis or classis assembly. The presbytery is also such a regional body.[2] Each parish delegates a minister and an elder to the presbytery. The moderator acts as the chair of the presbytery, comparable with the chair of the classis. Both the classis and the presbytery convene several times a year on a regular basis. As regional bodies they function in between the consistories or sessions on the one hand and the regional and/or general synods or the synod and the general assembly on the other hand.

---

[1] Janssen/Van den Broeke, *A Collegial Bishop*; Van den Broeke, *Classis in crisis*; Van den Broeke, *Een geschiedenis van de classis*; accessed 11 March 2020. http://www.kerkrecht.nl/node/5951.

[2] Hall, *Jus Divinum Regiminis Ecclesiastici*; General Assembly, *The Practice*.

Classis and presbyteries are everywhere in the world where Reformed and Presbyterian denominations are. For example, in 2016 I came across several plaques when I visited the remembrance place of the Danish Lutheran missionary Ludwig Ingwer Nommensen (1834-1918) on Sumatra. He was the founder of the HKBP, the *Huria Kristen Batak Protestan*. People visit this place like a spiritual pilgrimage. These plaques reveal that people from local churches come here for an ecclesial and/or spiritual retreat. They do not only mention the name of their church or group, but also the name of their classis, like in this picture I took of a plaque which mentions the spiritual retreat of the church of Kolose of the Classis Katipa belonging to the GBKP, the *Gereja Batak Karo Protestan* or the *Karo Batak Protestant Church*.

Plaque at the Nommensen remembrance centre on Sumatra, Indonesia (photographer: Leon van den Broeke)[3]

---

3 I thank Lenta Enni Simbolon for her help with the translation and providing further information.

This book is not a plea for putting church polity in the spotlights. The authors are aware of the fact that church polity alone does not save, but it might protect. Church polity does not constitute the house of what we call the church, but nonetheless it can be considered as the rafters. It is about the theological understanding of the church as it manifests, or ought to manifest (regional) catholicity. But how can the classis or the presbytery manifest regional catholicity? The classis or the presbytery can be considered as body of Christ. In it both the new testament notions of *episkopē* (supervision) and *koinōnia* (fellowship) are or can be present. Sometimes the daily practice conflicts with the ideal of fellowship and/or the proper execution of *episkopē*. Also, the idea of the classis as an assembly is today in the shadow of the classis as a platform. In the Preface René de Reuver pictured the renewed classis in the PCN in this way: as a platform 'where the congregations will meet and where they will be responsible for building each other up in faith, in hope, in love'.[4] The role of the classis in terms of dealing with both doctrinal and ethical issues is hardly present. When the church at regional level is polarized and suffers from plurality, scarcely any fellowship remains. In such a case the sense of the classis as a manifestation of catholicity fades. Catholicity requires an answer to the difficult question how office-bearers and/or the local churches overcome and live with their differences.

That touches upon the topic of authority and how to use authority in a fruitful way. The interesting dimension of Janssen's contribution is that he focusses both on the relationship between the local churches and the classis, and sharpens his focus by reflecting on the authority of the classis in relation to the general synod or assembly. Thereby his primary focus is his statement that governing authority has to do with the type of leading the church that it conforms to be a *gestalte* of the Kingdom of God. His interest in relative authority has to do with an understanding of church order, namely how authority is 'distributed' among the various parties: office, assemblies, congregations, church members. He states: "Granted that original, and final, authority comes from God and God's self-revelation, authority comes in different guises. Ministers of the Word have an authority to proclaim the Word to a congregation and to administer the sacraments."[5]

When the theological notion of the classis is lost, then the classis and the presbytery are no more than platforms or nothing more than administrative and/or managerial bodies; when they are only about governance, and not

---
4 See page 18.
5 See page 27.

about proclaiming the gospel, they do not function as the engines which John Chalmers aims for. The presbytery can be or become the engine of the church, but then a transition according to the above-mentioned process is necessary. It connects with what Joseph D. Small states. He writes that when the presbytery became a managerial body people no longer talk about 'us', but about 'them'. It is an indication of the sense of lost fellowship. Small writes about managerial bodies which are forms without substance, tolerance, and institutional forbearance. According to Small the point of departure for renewal of mutual tolerance and institutional forbearance is 'the renewed attention to what polity itself is intended to accomplish'. This includes recovery of the purposes of '*episkopē* – oversight – especially the *episkopē* exercised by presbyteries', Small states.[6]

Whereas Small shares his ecclesiological and church polity concern with view to the managerial bodies and how (church) polity dies, another North-American theologian, Kathleen S. Smith, writes about the changing situation with view to the classis in the Christian Reformed Church in North America (CRCNA), not only when it comes to the nature of the classis, but also concerning the roles of classical functionaries. These changes make the CRCNA classis more equipped for the twenty-first-century context, as Smith states. However, it comes with a price. Coming from the Reformed type of classis the renewal is the result of a specific taskforce: Classis Renewal Team which responds to the need of the classes in the CRCNA. Smith states that recently many classes in the CRCNA are in the process of learning to understand the nature of classis as *koinōnia*. It means that the classis has shifted from a body of delegated office-bearers to do the ecclesiastical business to a platform that worships, learns together, encourages fellowship and care, and sponsors regional ministries. That is encouraging and promising. It seems an extension of what Article 32 of the DCO stated: every gathering of the assemblies of the church needs to begin with calling the Name of the Lord and closed with saying grace.[7] This means more than just saying a prayer at the beginning and the end of every meeting. It implies that all the acts (In Dutch: 'handelingen') of these bodies will be executed in a divine atmosphere. It's not like running a (church) business. So, who would have difficulties with the longing in the CRCNA classes for more devotion? As

---

6 See page 112.
7 In seventeenth-century Dutch: "De handelinghen aller t'samen-comsten sullen met aenroepinghe des Naems Gods aenghevanghen / ende met een danckseginghe besloten worden;" accessed 19 March 2020, http://www.kerkrecht.nl/node/471.

this is said, the question raises, what this means for the notion of supervision of the classis. The plea for more *koinōnia* also questions the presence of and need for *episkopē* in the same divine sphere. Still, some CRCNA classes show resistance to the changes and prefer to maintain the episcopal notion of the classis. They are reluctant to the renewal of the classis and want to maintain the Reformed tradition.

History shows that it is hard for denominations to find a proper balance. The same goes for new contexts. They do not only have consequences for the classis or presbytery as a body or middle judicatory, but also for a supralocal office-bearer, like the so-called *classispredikant* in the PCN. Klaas-Willem de Jong focusses in his contribution on the *classispredikant*, the classis minister, in the PCN. In 2018 this type of pastor was installed. There are eleven of those pastors. Each functions in one of the eleven enlarged classes. Until 1 May 2018 there have been 74 (smaller) classes. The focal point of the *classispredikant* demonstrates that the (new) classis in the PCN is not only about being a platform, but touches on the issue of *episkopē* at the classis level, and in this case of the *classispredikant*. This is embedded in the classis renewal of 2018 as a result of the decision of the General Synod of the PCN to be(come) a simpler church, with less administration and less bureaucratism. This process of renewal has not only ecclesial developments as motive, but also societal developments, like digitalization, globalization, glocalization and de-institutionalization. These developments challenge the churches tremendously and this has its consequences for the existence and functioning of the classis and the presbytery. Problems in or with the classis and the presbytery are mostly expressions or symptoms of underlying and other problems, both ecclesial and societal. One should not forget the ecclesiological notion of the classis and the presbytery. Usually they do not receive much ecclesiological, more ecclesial, and hardly any societal attention. Classis as corporate action is important, the same goes for renewal, but ecclesiological reflection on the four notions of the church (one, holy, catholic and apostolic) cannot be missed. One of the outcomes was the installation of the *classispredikant* as from 1 May 2018. In an interesting way De Jong compares the *classispredikant* with the moderator of the United Reformed Church (URC) in the United Kingdom. He concludes that this classis minister is 'at most half a bishop; however, he does have the potential to develop into an almost whole one'.[8]

---

8 See page 68.

This raises the question whether this is a good development or not. It does not only reveal something about the nature or development of the classis minister itself, but also about the nature of the classis. As might have become clear by now another result of the ecclesial renewal project Church 2025 in the PCN was the reduction from 74 smaller classes to 11 larger classes. I highlight this development, its history and consequences. These 11 classes have, so to speak, more the size of the former particular synods than of the classes. Anyhow, it questions (again) the balance between on the one hand fellowship and on the other hand supervision, as there is little understanding of the nature and the importance of the classis for today's church life. If office-bearers take an interest in the life and the work of the classis it is for the notion of the classis as a platform, to exchange ideas, to experience fellowship, and to share best practices. Still, the classis needs in some way or the other something of *episkopē*. Moreover, its very nature is to execute both *episkopē*, in a collegial way, and *koinōnia* – as it is a body of neighboring (local) churches. In my contribution I yield *koinōnia* and show that the classis in whatever format cannot function without supervision to be a buffer to today's individualism of local churches and a safeguard for (regional) catholicity.

Surprisingly another example of how the classis developed and operates today comes from the Czech Republic. Adam Csukás is the author of a contribution which deals with the question whether the Evangelical Church of Czech Brethren (ECCB) has a Presbyterian church polity, which traditionally attributes importance to the classis as the key judicatory of the denomination. Therefore he focusses on the characteristics of the (historical development of the) church polity of the ECCB. This includes the impact of historical and local circumstances on the church polity of this denomination and of its predecessors. Against this church polity context he explains the nature of the classis within the ECCB. His contribution highlights an awareness which is more present in the Central-European context than elsewhere, namely the political context and influence on church governance. It became apparent in the parity between both the state and the church when it comes to church governance. It means that every level of church governance requires two representatives, namely, the minister and the curator who is – in Hungarian and Slovak – an 'overseer' or 'guardian', in other words, *episkopos*. In comparison with the classis (renewal) in the CRCNA it is intriguing to see a similar increase in awareness in the ECCB with view to the importance and therefore renewal of the classis in the document 'Reformanda 2030: The Strategic Plan of the ECCB'. This concerns less emphasis on fellowship, and more on supervision of the classical committees and classical assemblies. Not only can the renewal or reform of the classis in the ECCB be pointed out, but also some similarity between the *classispredikant* in the Dutch PCN and the *senior* or the Synodical *Senior* in the ECCB.

Again, Csukás' contribution highlights a historical, political and societal awareness, but he is not the only one. John Chalmers seems to give account of the political context of the historical dimension and development to church polity. Moreover, his contribution even starts with it, although he points out also to the doctrinal standards or confessions of faith in Scotland. At least, in his contribution he pictures the complex history of the emergence of Presbyterian government. Furthermore, it explores ways in which the classis or the presbytery itself might recover some of its original potency and, in particular, its role as a *bishop* in the church. Chalmers has certain preferences when it comes to the very nature of such a bishop: more supportive than competitive, more concerned with compassion than with discipline, more driven by grace than by law, and more focused on the spiritual well-being of the members of the presbytery than on getting through the business.

As mentioned before, someone said at the conference: "The classis is more under pressure than I thought." We expect that in the upcoming ten years the classis and the presbytery will be under even more pressure than in the past decennium. The classis and the presbytery will suffer from greater pressure, other ecclesial and/or managerial problems, and societal developments. But this is not the only story to tell. The big question for churches and ecclesial policy makers is how to bring classis and the presbytery to faith and to life, and how to support each other in the resort of the classis and presbytery, and how to deal with plurality. The answer is not to reduce the classis or presbytery to a platform, and also not limit it to its episcopal function. Moreover, they cannot be saved by considering them as only managerial bodies. The theological notion of the classis and presbytery should not be forgotten. Their nature needs to be re-discovered and re-understood in the light of mutual toleration and institutional forbearance for the sake of the Gospel and the well-being of the church and its members. In the context of globalization, nationalism and (g)localization also the notion of being church in the region should not be lost. Regional bodies as the classis and presbytery can still help local churches and denominations to be church today, in a process of turbulent transition, without forgetting its traditions.

Who knows that within another ten years a new conference and/or volume on the classis and presbytery is required and needs a follow-up which includes other denominations and/or countries, as this second volume also includes new perspectives from the classis in the Czech Republic and the presbytery in Scotland, or even that such a volume includes best practices. For the moment the authors hope that the current book will help those who reflect on the classis and the presbytery in theology, those who are in charge of such bodies and those who are representatives to these bodies and try to participate and understand its very nature with the aim to help to edify the (local) church and to express at regional level something from the catholicity as the church is a *gestalte* of the Kingdom of God.

Bibliography

General Assembly. *The Practice of the Free Church of Scotland in her Several Courts*. 8th ed. Edinburgh: Knox Press, 1995.

Hall, David W., eds. *Jus Divinum Regiminis Ecclesiastici or the Divine Right of Church-Governement, orginally asserted by the Ministers of Sion College*. London, December 1646, Dallas TX: Naphtali Press, 1995.

Janssen, Allan J., and Leon van den Broeke, eds. *A Collegial Bishop: Classis and Presbytery at Issue*. Grand Rapids MI: Wm. B. Eerdmans, 2010 (*The Historical Series in the Reformed Church in America* 66).

Van den Broeke, Leon. *Classis in crisis: Om de classicale toekomst*. Zoetermeer: Boekencentrum, 2009.

Van den Broeke, C. [Leon]. *Een geschiedenis van de classis: Classicale typen tussen idee en werkelijkheid 1571-2004*. Kampen: Kok, 2005.

Digital sources
http://www.kerkrecht.nl/node/5951

Who Says? The Authority of the Classis/Presbytery in a Reformed Church

Allan Janssen

The book that resulted from the conference held ten years ago on the classis/presbytery had its title *A Collegial Bishop?* in the interrogative.[1] The collected essays offered a qualified yes in response. It was qualified because the classis performs certain episcopal functions. In the recent round of the North American Reformed-Roman Catholic dialogue, partners from the Roman church acknowledged that the Reformed churches indeed maintain a certain episcopal structure. But the answer is only qualified because the classis/presbytery does not perform all the functions of an episcopate or does not do so in the manner of the episcopate historically manifest.

The conference of 2018 was designed to explore the nature and function of the classis[2] within a Reformed understanding of the nature of the church. I will shape this contribution around the question of the relative *authority* of the classis within a Reformed or Presbyterian church. I do so because one way of understanding church order is how authority is 'distributed' among the various parties: office, assemblies, congregations, church members. Granted that original, and final, authority comes from God and God's self-revelation, authority comes in different guises. Ministers of the Word have an authority to proclaim the Word to a congregation and to administer the sacraments. Governing authority is of a different kind; it has to do with leading the church in such a way that the church conforms to what it is meant to be, a *gestalte* of the kingdom of God. And that is what primarily is in focus in this paper.

I will sharpen my focus by reflecting on the authority of the classis in relation to the general synod or assembly. I will note how authority functions in the other 'direction' in the relation of the classis to the consistory or session. I will emphasize the former because it has been the

---

1 Janssen/Van den Broeke, *A Collegial Bishop?*
2 I will use the term 'classis' to denote both classis and presbytery.

subject of tension, even church division, throughout the history of the Reformed churches.

Two examples should make the point. The first is with the *Algemeen Reglement*, the 'General Regulations', in the Nederlandse Hervormde Kerk. The church order instituted by King Willem I in 1816 following the establishment of the Kingdom of the Netherlands, limited the authority of the general synod. The synod was not authorized to adjudicate doctrinal differences, although it was charged with the 'maintenance of its doctrine'. This led to years of struggle within that church, to say nothing of divisions in the church itself.[3]

A second illustration comes from my own church, the Reformed Church in America (RCA). In the latter part of the nineteenth century, a number of churches composed of recently immigrated persons protested to the General Synod the fact that members of secret societies were allowed to be members of Reformed churches. The synod responded by saying that while it agreed with the complainants, it was not within the synod's authority to direct boards of elders on this matter. Church membership remained within the purview of a local board of elders.[4] While neither of these instances are about a conflict between the classis and the synod, they illustrate the issue of how authority is distributed within the church.

A Church Reformed
Before I discuss the issue of authority, however, I offer a very attenuated sketch of how the Reformed have understood the nature of the church – or one version of it anyway. I could cite a number of places, but the Heidelberg Catechism will suffice, where in answer to Question 54, 'What do you believe concerning the holy catholic church?' the catechism puts it that

> the Son of God through his Spirit and Word, out of the entire human race, from the beginning of the world to its end, gathers, protects, and preserves for himself a community chosen for eternal life and united in true faith. And of this community I am and always will be a living member.

Note first that the church is a community or congregation (*gemeinde* in the original, which can also be translated as church.) The church is not identified with a hierarchy, nor with an institution as such, but with a communion of persons constituted by the trinitarian God. As Herman

---

3 On this see, e.g., Blei, *The Netherlands Reformed Church*, 57–58.
4 See Janssen, "An Abstract Question?"

Bavinck put it: "The church (...) is especially a this-worldly term, a fellowship of persons equipped with offices and ministries that function in the visible world as the gathered people of God."[5]

But how does the Son 'gather, protect, and preserve'? We know this through the well-known marks of the church articulated by John Calvin: the right proclamation of the Word and the correct use of the sacraments, to which the later Reformed would add a third mark, that of discipline. This would become a mantra of the Reformed churches: the church is a *creatura Verbi*, a creation of the Word. And if the sacraments have too often faded from view with some, perhaps even many, Reformed theologians and churches, it is Christ's presence in the sacraments as well as through the Word, that gathers believers at the Lord's own table.

But I will stay with proclamation for the moment, for that will further our story when we turn to the question of authority. Abraham (Bram) van de Beek traces the tale like this (and here we're on the trail of the classis as bishop). He begins with Ignatius, where the bishop stood as the guarantee of the truth of the gospel. The church was to be unified in doctrine, and doctrine was about the gospel itself. When the story turns to Cyprian, the issue is the authority of the bishop. But on what basis did that authority rest? The bishop was appointed by neighboring bishops. It was to be in a communion of bishops. Then we turn to Calvin, who was not himself opposed to bishops, but for whom Cyprian's measure no longer worked. The marks were, as noted above, the proclamation of the Word and the right use of the sacraments. However, they did not stand alone. Ministry was the key. While ministry was not essential to the church, not of the *esse* of the church, the Word was proclaimed and the sacraments administered through ministry as God's instrument.[6]

There is one more thing to notice from Answer 54 of the Catechism. The Son gathers, protects, etc. the church through Word and *Spirit*. The church is the work of the Spirit. While the Spirit works in conjunction with the Word, the Spirit engages where it will. The Spirit manifests the freedom of God, and that includes God's freedom *vis a vis* the structures of the church.

We are not yet, of course, at the place where we can discuss classes or even synods. They weren't around with Calvin.[7] But neither were bishops

---

5 Bavinck, *Reformed Dogmatics* IV, 298.
6 Van de Beek, "The Dis-Unity of the Reformed Churches," 109–120.
7 Although Geneva had a proto-type of the classis in the *Vénérable Compagnie des Pasteur*. See Van den Broeke, "The History of the Classis," 17–18.

in the Reformed churches. So to the development of another means, that of the assemblies. That has its own history.[8] However, it is important to note another factor in the Reformed understanding of the church. This was its anti-hierarchical character.[9] This feature can be seen as a reaction to the accretion of power by Rome. But theologically, it is the freedom of the Word to form the church in each locality, the Word proclaimed in both preaching and sacrament. Hence the famous first article of the church order of Emden: "No church shall have precedence or rule over another, no minister over minister, no elder over elder, no deacon over deacon, but rather each will be alert for all suspicion thereof and occasion thereto."[10] In that regard we note that first Wesel and then Emden used the phrase 'neighboring churches'[11] to denote what would later become classes (in the churches with the Dort Church Order (DCO) order as heritage).

Episcopal authority
What then of authority? As we noted, the Reformed were wary of – nay even allergic to – hierarchical authority as it was expressed in the Roman church. But they were also wary of the kind of enthusiastic forms of authority that was finding expression among the free churches of the Anabaptist sort. So, they would set up a system of assemblies. But they were careful to allot authority carefully. Article 30 of the DCO puts it clearly:

> In those Assemblies, ecclesiastical *matters* only shall be transacted, and in an ecclesiastical manner. A greater Assembly shall take cognition of those things alone which could not be determined in a lesser, or that appertain to the churches or congregations in general, who compose such an assembly.

How is this authority then distributed between the classes and the General Synod? I will take as example my own church, allowing for differences in other churches, differences that, by the way, illustrate the nature of the issue. In the relation between the classes and the General Synod, authority resides in the classis in this way. To take the example of my own church, the classis has as its responsibilities:

---

8   See Van den Broeke, "The History of the Classis," 9–46.
9   For example, the Church Order of Emden, 1571, Article 1.
10 Acts Synod of Emden, Article 1. *Kerkelijk Handboek*.
11 Ibid.

- the examination and ordination of ministers of Word and sacrament;
- the commissioning of elders either as preaching elders or as commissioned pastors;
- the supervision and discipline of ministers of Word and sacrament;
- the formation and disbanding of local churches;
- general superintendence of local churches;
- all authority not granted other assemblies of the church.

Particularly to be noted here is responsibility for the integrity of the proclamation of the gospel, or to use Van de Beek's terms, the 'unity of doctrine'. The classis alone has the authority to determine the admission of persons to the pulpits. It does so as it examines candidates for ministry, and indeed can examine ministers, even from other Reformed churches, who are candidates for a pulpit within the classis. Moreover, the classis also determines who will preside at table in the local churches, thereby manifesting its place in the apostolic task of the church. Furthermore, in its superintendence, it oversees local boards of elders in their responsibilities as the classis enquires both about the integrity of the proclamation of the gospel and for the elder's responsibility in the administration of the sacraments. This is the expression of authority in the direction of the consistories or sessions.

Three things are of relevance to our theme. First, as gathered offices, that is, as those who are ordained to come *to* the church as representatives of Christ, the offices deliberate as they are led by the Word. The Son of God gathers, protects, etc. And the Son does so through the instrument of ministry, in this case ministry gathered in council.

Second, deliberation is done in council. The Reformed aversion both to hierarchy and to the leadership of the charismatic individual emerges particularly here. No individual office-bearer can act in the stead of the gathered offices — except where authorized by the body to execute its actions. Furthermore, it is in council where the Spirit blows freely.

Third, the classis consists not only of ministers of the Word, but also includes elders. Elders are at the heart of a Reformed polity. As Oepke Noordmans once remarked, the elder is the 'pawn' that checkmated the Roman pope.[12] The elder is an office that lives and works among the people of God, and so gives voice to those shaped by the Word in the midst of everyday life. This, too, is anti-hierarchical. More importantly,

---

12 Noordmans, *Verzamelde Werken* 5, 398.

the classis includes the elder in the discernment of God's intentions with and for the church.

One more thing is to be noted about the classis. In contradistinction from the synods, the classis is *local*. It consists of members and delegates from neighboring churches. In practice, this means that classes as bodies live and work together over periods of time. This allows for two things. One, the body can deliberate over an extended period of time. This is crucial, since discernment of what the Spirit is leading through the Word is not always ready to hand. Second, as local office-bearers who continue to live and work together, their life together allows for accountability. (This is particularly the case in matters of discipline. The body, the classis – like a board of elders – must live with its decisions. Indeed, office-bearers must live with each other when they *differ* in coming to decision).

As with all assemblies, the General Synod's authority is limited. Decisions of the General Synod do have import for the proclamation of the Word and the celebration of the sacraments in an indirect, albeit real, way. While the synod has no magisterial authority – it cannot on its own determine the teaching of the church – it can propose changes to the constitutional structure of the church, which includes confessional changes as well as changes to the liturgy and the polity. More importantly, the seminaries and the theological education agency are agents of the synod. The synod has oversight in what is being taught in the seminaries (although as seminaries become more ecumenical in their faculties, this power has been considerably diluted). The RCA has also retained the office of the professor, and the professor is amenable to the synod for what she or he teaches. So the synod exercises some authority in setting the standards by which candidates for ministry receive their 'certificate for fitness' which is their 'ticket' for admission to the ordination examination by the classis.

I mentioned that the practice of authority differs some in other Reformed churches. I'll take two North American churches as illustration. The first is the Presbyterian Church (U.S.A.). Their general assembly can offer an 'authorized interpretation'. The responsibilities of the General Assembly include that it is to 'nurture the covenant community of the disciples of Christ' and that shall include (…) authoritatively interpreting the most recent edition of the *Book of Order* in accordance with the provision of G-6.02[13] or through a decision of the General Assembly Permanent Judicial Commission in a remedial or disciplinary case, with the most recent interpretation of the *Book of Order* being binding (…).[14]

One notes, however, that this authority is clearly circumscribed and is limited to the interpretation of the *Book of Order*.

The situation is a bit different in the CRCNA. Their synod has the authority to adopt creeds, alter the polity, and change elements in worship. However, it can do so only upon 'prior consideration of the churches'.[15] Moreover while their church order reflects Article 30 of the DCO in that the major assemblies make decisions that are not within the purview of the minor assemblies, the decisions of the assemblies are considered 'settled and binding'.[16]

The synods, like the classes, are themselves assemblies or councils of the church, composed of ministers and elders (and sometimes deacons). Like the classes, they deliberate together, and together they discern how the Spirit may be leading the church. However, the synods are not local. Nor are they in practice a continuing body.[17] This means that in fact very little real Biblical discernment takes place. A meeting of a few days, where delegates are limited to two-minutes to offer their wisdom, scarcely offers sufficient time for deliberation. What has evolved is a parliamentary process whereby a simple majority 'discerns' the will of God for the church! This has led to political maneuvering from whatever interest wishes to effect its point of view (always convinced, of course, that their point of view is God's!).[18]

---

13 *Book of Order: Constitution of the Presbyterian Church (U.S.A.) Part 2*, G-6.02, oga. pcusa.org_site_media/media/uploads/oga/pdf/book-of-order2017-electronic.pdf, accessed October 15, 2018 (Hereafter *Book of Order*). G-6.02 concerns the composition of an "Advisory Committee on the Constitution
14 *Book of Order*, G-3.0501c.
15 Christian Reformed Church in North America, *Church Order and Its Supplements*, Article 47 and Supplement, www.crcna.org/sites/default/files/1017_church_order.pdf, accessed October 15, 2018 (Hereafter *Church Order*).
16 *Church Order*, Articles 28b, 29.
17 Technically, at least in the RCA, the synod is a continuing body. However, financial and geographical restraints mean that it almost never meets more that for a few days in a year.
18 This is particularly evident in matters of discipline, where synod delegates rarely have to live together with either the disciplined or with one another.

Thus far it appears as though the weight of authority tends toward the classis. However, the general synod/assembly is not without authority in relation to the classis. As a geographical entity, the interests of a classis can focus locally in disregard to the broader responsibilities of the church. As the church is gathered in synod, it can take cognizance of the greater responsibilities of the church. The synod can 'set a course' (it is a *synod*, 'together on the way'). This can be illustrated by a responsibility given the Presbyterian Church (U.S.A.) in its government where, under the rubric of providing 'that the Word of God may be truly preached and heard', it includes 'establishing a comprehensive mission strategy and priorities for the church'.[19]

Problems

This division of authority has its own set of problems. I will illustrate from my own church and I will focus on the issue of infant baptism. A number of classes, influenced primarily by ministers educated outside Reformed seminaries, have allowed congregations to practice infant dedication in the stead of infant baptism, a clear violation of the confessions of the church. Another classis, observing and disturbed by the practice, has no recourse when a classis violates or ignores the church's confessional commitments. The General Synod has no authority to intervene, save in a judicial case.

The fundamental issue in Reformed polity, as I see it, is the nature of the synod itself. The church is not a denominational institution. Denominational 'structures' are an epiphenomenon. That is, they are put into place to do the work of the synod. But the synod is nothing more than the gathering of the offices, which is, in fact, a gathering of the classes. What holds them together is a common confession. (That, in turn, is not simply agreement in doctrine, but a unified acknowledgement of the One whose presence is gospel). The church holds together as synod only so long as they can gladly confess together. This of course has been a problem that has often enough been pointed out.[20]

By this illustration, it is clear that a local classis can become captive to its secular or even ecclesiastical culture. This can have immediate effect on, say, those whom it will ordain. A candidate whose theological perspective falls well within the bounds of the church's confessions can be

---

19 *Book of Order,* G-3.0501a.
20 See, e.g., Smit, "Confessions as Instruments of (Dis)unity."

denied ordination on non-confessional grounds. This is often felt most clearly by minority, often ethnic minority, churches within classes.

This further indicates that there may be no final court of appeal when classis (the 'bishop') errs. Of course, redress always exists, but the course is such that the appeal to redress begins from within the classis. Now, the 'solution' to this is that the church confesses together. That is the classes come together as they 'sign on' to a set of what we call 'standards of unity'. But that works only so long as it works!

This has led to an odd state of affairs brought on by confusion over the relation between the classes and the synod. Some classes have desired the synod to have authority to declare what is legitimate within the church. But classes have also be jealous of their own authority – and often it is the same classes that desired the synod to 'take hold'. So we are left with a dilemma. I suggest that such is a dilemma that the church order cannot resolve given the nature of the church.

And there is a further problem, already indicated in the above. The Reformed reacted to governance by individual persons because of the potential of the individual to act on his or her own and not by the guidance of the Spirit. Governance by council is thought to be a guard against such tyranny. However, councils, especially local councils, can be as tyrannical as individuals. Little keeps a group from prejudice. It is easy to devolve into governance by a 'majority', what the American founding fathers, in the Federalist Papers, called the 'tyranny of the majority'.

So far as I can see, there is no church order 'solution' to these problems. That may be a matter for further study and reflection. However, in my opinion, we are at a place where the issue is not the order itself, but that the church listen together to its Lord, to the one who indeed 'gathers, protects', etc. The church order is itself the product of the church listening to its Lord. But it also exists to enable the church to listen together thereby to live and act in obedience. The church does not govern itself but is ruled by the One who uses the ministry as instruments. The issue is the extent to which the church is obedient. The order of the church attempts to shape the church in such a way that it remains a church that listens to its Lord. But it cannot guarantee the same. It can only live in mutual accountability that ultimately remains accountable to the One who in joyful fact 'preserves for himself a community'.

Bibliography

Bavinck, Herman. *Reformed Dogmatics* IV, trans. John Vriend. Grand Rapids: Baker Academic, 2008.

Blei, Karel. *The Netherlands Reformed Church 1571-2005*, trans. Allan J. Janssen. Grand Rapids: Eerdmans, 2006.

Book of Order: Constitution of the Presbyterian Church (U.S.A.), oga.pcusa.org_site_media/media/uploads/oga/pdf/book-of-order2017-electronic.pdf, accessed October 15, 2018 (Hereafter *Book of Order*). G-6.02 concerns the composition of an Advisory Committee on the Constitution.

Christian Reformed Church in North America. *Church Order and Its Supplements*, Article 47 and Supplement, www.crcna.org/sites/default/files/1017_church_order.pdf, accessed October 15, 2018 (Hereafter *Church Order*).

Janssen, Allan J. "An Abstract Question? On the Authority of the General Synod." *Perspectives*, March/April, 2013.

Janssen, Allan J., and Leon van den Broeke. *A Collegial Bishop? Classis and Presbytery at Issue.* Grand Rapids: Eerdmans, 2010.

Kerkelijk Handboek. Kampen: Zalmen, 1882.

Noordmans, O. *Verzamelde Werken* V. Kampen: Kok, 1984.

Smit, Dirkie. "Confessions as Instruments of (Dis)unity)." In Eduardus Van der Borght, ed., *The Unity of the Church: A Theological State of the Art and Beyond.* Leiden: Brill, 2010.

Van de Beek, A. "The Dis-Unity of the Reformed Churches." In Lukas Vischer, ed., *The Church in Reformed Perspective: A European Reflection.* Geneva: s.n., 2002, 109–120 (*John Knox Series* 13).

Van den Broeke, Leon. "The History of the Classis." In Allan J. Janssen and Leon van den Broeke, eds., *A Collegial Bishop? Classis and Presbytery at Issue.* Grand Rapids MI: Eerdmans, 2010, 9–46.

For What Reason is the Classis on Earth? The Classis as a Buffer between Ecclesial Individualism and Regional Catholicity in the Context of Globalization, Regionalism and Glocalization

LEON VAN DEN BROEKE

Introduction
On 1 April 2018 Allan Janssen, General Synod Professor of the Reformed Church of America, and I organized a conference at the New Brunswick Theological Seminary. The title of conference was: 'A Collegial Bishop? The Classis and Presbytery at Issue'. Despite the fact that the topic was not hot, and that the regional ecclesiastical structure gets far less attention than the local church and the denomination, between 60 and 70 people attended the conference and experienced a common understanding and a good spirit. The classis and the presbytery are relevant for the denominations involved as the region can be regarded as 'sozialer und kirchlicher Handlungsraum' – the region as a social and ecclesial space to act – as the German theologian Karl-Fritz Daiber has stated.[1] He begins his contribution by pointing out that social connections are bound to a certain space. However this social space has changed over times. The same could then be said for the classis and the presbytery. The above-mentioned remark, about less attention, does not refer to historical studies on the classes; I refer, rather, to publications with a view to the present and future of the classis. Although by nature historical in character, the article of the Dutch professor in religious history Fred van Lieburg is one of the exceptions, if not the only one.[2] In 2010 the conference proceedings of the above-mentioned international conference

---
1 Daiber, "Die Region als sozialer und kirchlicher Handlungsraum," 15-46.
2 Van Lieburg, "Van classicale organisatie tot civil society," 78–83.

were published.³ Since then not only has society and the political context changed, but the ecclesial context as well, not only in the Netherlands, but also in the United States of America, South Africa, Indonesia, Australia, New Zealand, Scotland, Hungary and wherever else classes and presbyteries exist. This gave rise to the thought of a follow up: 'A Collegial Bishop Revisited? The Classis and Presbytery at Issue'. This is also influenced by recent developments in the classical structure in the Protestant Church in the Netherlands, because due to the ecclesial renewal project called *Kerk 2025* this structure has been re-organized. Already in 2009 I paid attention to the crisis in the classical structure in my book *Classis in crisis*, but I also kept an eye on best practices.⁴ The effects of the renewal project in the Protestant Church in the Netherlands, *Kerk 2025*, is at least threefold: first, a great deal of attention for the regional structure of the church, since usually the local church and the denomination attract much more attention in both the church and theology. Second, the reduction from 74 to 11 classes with the focus on *koinōnia*; and third a slightly episcopal transition: the installation of 11 *classispredikanten* – classis ministers. Therefore, the question is how the classical reorganization in the PCN effects the ecclesiological and ecclesiastical notions of and in the eleven new classes against the backdrop of the changing societal and political context.

From a terminological point of view, I make a distinction between the classis as the entity of several congregations mostly in a certain region (although in some cases non-geographical classes might exist) and the classis assembly as the gathering of office-bearers delegated by their consistories which is in charge of governing the classis for the benefit of both the local churches and the denomination.⁵

This contribution has the following paragraphs to provide one or more answers to the question in the concluding paragraph. First I will address the church renewal project of the PCN called *Kerk 2025*. The second paragraph will deal with the implications for the nature of the classis (as a community of several congregations in a certain region) and the classis assembly (the middle-judicatory). The third paragraph is on the classis assembly as an ecclesiological buffer between the consistories on the one hand and the general synod on the other hand. The fourth paragraph focusses on the influence of the increasing mobility due to the

---

3 Janssen/Van den Broeke, *A Collegial Bishop*.
4 Van den Broeke, *Classis in Crisis*.
5 Van den Broeke, "Non-Geographic Classes?," 51–68.

railway infrastructure constructed between 1839 and 1939 in the Netherlands and its effects on the community of the church. The fifth paragraph moves forward to the present and past landscape, more specifically: the *polder*, in the Netherlands and the related Dutch mentality. It includes six virtues of the Netherlands. These are applied to the classis assembly and the classis. The last paragraph is the concluding paragraph.

Kerk 2025 and the classis
The former secretary-general of the general synod of the PCN, Arjan Plaisier, took the initiative for this project. He considered five societal developments that are important for the (development of the) church: a secular society, individual choices, a network society, digital revolution, and globalization.[6] These developments challenge the church in whatever country or region around the globe, including the Netherlands.

Furthermore, he stated that too much time and energy in the church is devoted to governance, and not to following Jesus. Plaisier had a big vision to reduce the institutional structure of the church, its procedures, rules and power, to focus more on discipleship, following Jesus, apostolate. This had consequences for the ecclesiastical organization. The nature of his reorganization was: simplicity, space, and transparency, but was more ecclesial than ecclesiological in nature; it is more the outcome of an ecclesial reflection than the result of a profound theological reflection about the nature of the church (ecclesiology).

Simplicity meant that there should be fewer procedures, rules, regulations and less focus on the institution of the church. Space meant that the church should yield more to the local church and fresh expressions of church (the so-called *pioniersplekken*). In November 2015 the general synod unanimously decided to accept the document 'Kerk 2025: Waar een Woord is, is een weg' ["Where there is a Word there is a Way"] as the theological foundation for elaboration and research with view to the policy of the PCN.

This synodical decision has also affected the organization of the 74 classes. According to the Synod of Emden of 1571 the classis is a community of neighboring churches.[7] This has implications for notions

---

6 Accessed 18 October 2018, https://www.protestantsekerk.nl/kerk2025/kerk2025#nota kerk2025.
7 "Classische versamelinghen van sommighe Kercken die by een ghelegen zyn," section 7 Acts of the Synod of Emden 1571.

like distances, travel, places to stay overnight, and the importance of the classis for the delegates: is it a real community, or not? As of 1 May 2018 there are no longer 74, but 11 classes. This means that the 11 classes are larger, and as a consequence, the geographical distance between the congregations in the classes has also become greater, as well as the distance from most of the congregations to the venue of the classis assembly. Moreover, the mental distance between the congregations and the classes has increased. This not only has to do with the geographical distance. From a foreign perspective it might look silly that the Dutch congregations which exist in such a small country have difficulties with relatively short geographical distances. In some cases, delegated office-bearers in North-America and South-Africa delegated have to take the plane to reach the venue. In such cases the frequency of the meetings of the classis assembly or presbytery is less than three or four times a year. According to Allan J. Janssen, it is still very rare in the US for a classis to meet more than four times a year. Twice a year was pretty much the norm for many years. In other cases the office-bearers have to drive a couple of hours to show up in time for the meetings. So, in comparison the Dutch office-bearers should not complain (too much). However, distances are not only something which can be considered in an objective, but also in a subjective way; it is in this sense that delegated office-bearers complain about the time it takes to reach the venue. This will increase on 1 May. This implies that the agenda of the classis assembly has better be good and attractive, otherwise delegates could decide to stay at home and/or choose to work in the local congregation.

There is another aspect which increases the mental distance. This has to do with the fact that not every consistory can delegate an office-bearer. In a strict sense it means that not all the congregations are represented in the classis assembly through their consistories and delegated office-bearers. From the considerations of the former 74 classes assemblies it appeared that many of them objected to this ecclesiastical idea. They stated that their voice will not be heard and they are right. Although it can be considered as something negative, especially when such statements are uttered in an emotional way, I consider it also as something positive. It is an expression of commitment. At the same time it cannot be ignored that one of the reasons that the general synod decided to adopt and implement *Kerk 2025* in the church was that in many classes many delegated office-bearers were absent and that congregations were not represented. It also implied that too few (other) office-bearers had to fulfil the many tasks of the classis assembly and also that in some case the quality of the work was at issue. From a more ecclesiological perspective it has to be added that the classis assembly is, as with the consistory and the synod, not a parliament. In a strict sense of the word there is no democracy in the church. The nature of the church is *Christocratic*: it is Christ's church. He rules his church. This does not exclude the voice of congregants or office-bearers, on the contrary, but (delegated) office-bearers convene to listen to Christ's voice, deliberate and take decisions.

In order to meet the objections that classes would be too large, the general synod decided to grant the classes the possibility of smaller entities created of several congregations within the classis. This is not something new, but dates back to the Netherlands Reformed Church which officially had the so-called *ring* [circle] and the Dutch Reformed Church in the Republic which was unofficially familiar with the so-called *lokaten* or *kreij[t]sen*.[8] Although their positions were different, to a certain extent they were subdivisions within the classes.

All this emphasizes the fact that the nature of the classis since 2018 is considered more as fellowship and as a platform than as supervision. It demonstrates that the notion of supervision is not popular, but also unknown. Not only congregants, but also many office-bearers focus more on fellowship and platform rather than on supervision. This is emphasized by *Kerk 2025*. However, the question is whether everybody has the same understanding of encounter, whether encounter is not idealized in the church, and whether encounter is the (only) goal of the church. Steven Shakespeare states:

> I believe the reason for this is that the kind of idealistic *koinonia* privileged by [ecumenical] documents such as *The Nature and Mission of the Church* brackets out the contested political processes which arrived at ideas of holiness, catholicity, unity and apostolicity in the first place. The notion that these ideas are delivered to us freshly minted from the hand of God, and then tarnished by our historical hands is not sustainable. Without a critical questioning of such Platonic assumptions, we will lapse into Gnosticism, a devaluing of creation, time and difference. And we will not be able to recognize the necessary role of conflict in shaping the identity of the church.[9]

---

8 Van den Broeke, *Een geschiedenis van de classis*, 92, 101–103.
9 Shakespeare, "A Community of the Question," 159.

Moreover by doing so the PCN makes too much of a distinction between supervision and fellowship as if fellowship can only be reached without supervision, and as if supervision excludes fellowship.

The so-called *classispredikant*, the classis minister, is also new. In the PCN, 11 classis ministers have been appointed and are at work. Generally speaking the function/task/authority of the *classispredikant* is to give shape to the responsibility of the classis assembly for the supervision of the congregations and the office-bearers, Ord. 4-16 of the church order of the PCN. In this contribution I will focus more on the classis than on this *classispredikant*.[10]

An ecclesiological buffer
From the perspective of church polity (system) the classis assembly has been and remains a buffer between independentism, the local church and the consistory on the one hand, and synodocracy, the denomination and the general synod on the other hand. In general there is in ecclesial life too much emphasis on both the local and on the national levels. This has implications for the notion of catholicity and it raises a question about the balance between ecclesial individualism and (regional) catholicity. With view to the latter: the general synod easily attracts the attention. Congregants engage more easily with the local than the supralocal church. Also, from the theological perspective, attention via congregational studies also focusses more on the local than on the supralocal level. This not only includes studies on the local church as such, but also on the fresh expressions of church which mean those new churches or congregations which are planted and have a different organization intended to reach those who are not a member of a church and which meets the changed cultural context. The PCN invests a lot in such fresh expressions of church, also due to the renewal project *Kerk 2025*.[11]

The missing piece is both the academic and the ecclesial focus on the regional level, in our case the classis assembly. This assembly is necessary to prevent too great an ecclesial gap between the local church and the fresh expressions of church and the church on the national level. From the ecclesiological dimension the classis assembly can be considered as the figurehead of the presbyterial-synodical system as it provides and functions as a buffer between the two levels. The ecclesiological notion of

---
10 For the *classispredikant* see pages 55-71.
11 Accessed 2 January 2019, https://www.lerenpionieren.nl/blogs-en-columns/mozaiek-van-kerkplekken/

the classis is necessary to prevent the consistories and their local churches in their tendency towards independentism and individualism. Moreover the notion of the classis is important to safeguard the catholicity of the church in the region. The local churches and their consistories need each other, can help each other and assist one another. It is not only ideally so, but is also the case in reality. However, local churches are often struggling and are (too) occupied with themselves and/or do not take an interest in neighbouring churches, let alone the greater church. This is striking in an era of the connected world with so many possibilities to communicate and to form a community. Geographical distances should not be a problem (anymore).

Mobility
In 2007 the book *Het liep op rolletjes: De eenwording van protestant-christelijk Nederland per rail 1839-1939* ["Running Like Clockwork: The Unification of the Protestant Netherlands by rail 1839-1939"] on the effects of the railway system on church life in the Netherlands in the nineteenth and twentieth century was released.[12] As a result of the railway infrastructure, new opportunities occurred with regard to distances, travel and time. Although not every city, let alone village, was connected with this infrastructure, it made journeys within the Netherlands shorter. Travelers had new possibilities to travel other than moving on foot, horseback, carriage or by a boat or a ship. This offered tremendous new opportunities for the connection and communication of churches. This book focusses on the unity of protestant-Christian Netherlands via the railway system between 1839 and 1939. It shows the importance of the openings the railway system provided to churches as for example in book chapters as 'From paper community to direct contact' (Annemieke Kolle),[13] and 'A community on the rails' (Annemarie Houkes),[14] and a subtitle like 'Seceders between anti-modernity and mobility' (Dick Kuiper).[15]

As a result of the new railway system, preachers could travel more easily through the Netherlands. It also changed the idea of distance and ecclesial geography. Especially between 1860 and 1889, many more new railways were constructed. Also, the classis was no longer a district or

---
12 Kuiper/Vree, *Het liep op rolletjes*.
13 Kolle, "Van papieren gemeenschap naar direct contact," 45–65.
14 Houkes, "Een gemeenschap op de rails," 67–79.
15 Kuiper, "'Tafel en bed was voor ons gereed'," 105–116.

geographical territory wherein people lived for the rest of their lives, but it became possible to be more easily connected. In some cases, it meant that it was also easier to reach the venue of the classis and therefore contribute to the notion of the classis as an ecclesial regional entity.

For what reason is the Netherlands on earth?
The above-mentioned railway infrastructure not only affected societal life, but also the ecclesial context. It is an example of the influence of a changing political and societal context. Nowadays, the churches have to deal with the effect of globalization and glocalization.[16] Sometimes they even suggest an alternative to economic globalization as Riccardo Nanini showed in his contribution 'A Catholic Alternative to Globalization? the Compagnia Delle Opere'.[17] The not only changing, but already changed societal, political and economic developments effect the way religions are instituted. Despite this effect for Christianity there is still 'the assumption that the communal dimension of religion expresses itself through *organization*', as Peter Beyer states.[18] Nonetheless the organization of churches is also challenged. It has never been easier to reach the venue of the classis assembly and at the same time the number of attendees has never been so small. On the one hand the world is a (digital) global village, and on the other hand people tend to seek comfort, to close the borders, to emphasize nationalism and regionalism. This is not necessarily bad or wrong, although it can have negative consequences. Regionalism would also mean the cultivation of regional languages or dialects, the translation of the Bible or a hymn book into such languages or dialects. From a cultural perspective regionalism or nationalism could also mean that more attention is paid to one's own culture, heritage and products, and that people are more aware and proud of their own region.

Where the notion of the nation is dead for the one, as a result of the globalization and the European Union, for the other it means that the nation is alive and tends toward nationalism. The birth and maturation of the European Union for example also influence these developments.

Recently a new book has been released: *Waarom is NL op aarde?* ["Why is the Netherlands on earth?'][19] Through the metaphor and historical reality of the so-called *polder* landscape of the Netherlands the authors detected six

---

16 Beyer, "Globalization and the Institutional Modeling of Religions," 167–187.
17 Nanini, "Catholic Alternative to Globalization?" 47–76.
18 Beyer, "Globalization," 173.
19 Van den Brink, *Waarom is NL op aarde?*

virtues and characteristics of the Netherlands and/or Dutch mentality: safety, equality, material things, freedom, honesty, and attention.

First, safety means that to protect land sea dikes were and are still needed. Not only did dikes need to be repaired, remain under constant supervision, but new dikes also needed to be built. Moreover, since the dramatic flood of 1953 a plan, the Deltaworks (*Deltawerken*), was implemented. These Deltaworks are a series of construction works to protect the inhabitants and the southwestern part of the Netherlands with dams, dikes, levees, locks, sluices, and even storm surge barriers. Furthermore, living below sea-level requires permanent attention to safety. Its reverse side is an increase of rules and regulations.

Second, in a polder everybody is equal. Every human being is needed to protect the land, the dikes and to fight against the sea(level). Although some might be higher in rank than others, a storm or flood makes no distinction between rich and poor, powerful and powerless. In a *polder* you need each other to take care of the common safety, and in order to do so, you need to negotiate, to discuss, defend your own standpoint, but also to give in sometimes.[20] The Dutch do not trust envisioned leadership. In the *polder* everybody is to a certain extent equal. One of the saying in the Netherlands is: just do normal (*doe maar gewoon*).

Third, material things. The process of creating a new *polder* is a material occasion. It is about the working of locks, mills, water, weather and wind. This pragmatic approach has also its reverse side: the Dutch catch less an eye for imagination.

Four, freedom. It means that water is not only a threat, but also a blessing. It grants opportunities to sail, to trade with other cities, provinces, and countries, and to explore the world. It gives space, a maritime infrastructure and a(n international) market. However, it had as negative consequences: colonialism. Nonetheless, the Netherlands was able to make use of the maritime infrastructure and to become a maritime nation.

Five, honesty. Both at sea and in the *polder* you need to take care of yourself and each other, not so much through a central board or an institution. Besides you need to rely on each other: an agreement is agreement.[21] That is important. It means that the Dutch are straight forward, direct, and as a result sometimes rude.

Six, attention. From the perspective of the *polder* its meaning is that people within the polder need to take care of each other. The polder is a

---

20 The Dutch verb is: to *polder*.
21 In Dutch: *afspraak is afspraak*.

geographical and a natural entity which is protected by dikes and water. The reverse side is that the people in the polder take less care of others who live outside the *polder*, and outside the borders of the *polders*, those who are strangers or foreigners.

Armies and navies
On the basis of the German philosopher of law Carl Schmitt (1888-1985), the Dutch philosopher Haroon Sheikh distinguished between marines and navies in the chapter 'Tussen wereldzee en vasteland'[22] ["Between the Sea and the Continent"]. For example: Russia feels connected with the territory – an army, while the Netherlands can be more considered as a navy. That means that a naval nation is more entrepreneurial, individualistic and cosmopolitan in nature.

The same goes then for the Dutch. They are entrepreneurial, outgoing, and cosmopolitan. At the same time they can be individualistic. This is expressed in several contexts. A small illustration: at the moment of the conference the movement of the marine base (*the Van Braam Houckgeestkazerne*) from Doorn in the middle of the Netherlands to Flushing in the southwestern part of the Netherlands was heavy debated. By car, it is less than 200 kilometers. Even for marines who travel and work around the globe the move is problematic, because it is to the other side of the Netherlands. About a year after the conference was held, it appeared that two third of the marines will resign if the state would decide to move base to Flushing. The alderman of the city of Flushing, Albert Vader, said that the negative attitude and utterances in the media damages the image of the city of Flushing and of the Province of Zeeland.[23]

Not only societal developments, but political developments as well form the context in which the denominations and its classical assemblies and presbyteries are modelled and reorganized and in which they operate to deal with daily affairs. The reduction of the number of classes in the PCN and the enlargement of the size of the new classes fits with a society of scaling up, economies of scale or expansion. This is especially not only in schools, hospitals, and in business, but also in politics.[24] In 2011 the Rutte I administration (prime minister Mark Rutte) decided to develop

---

22 Sheikh, "Tussen wereldzee en vasteland," 211–232.
23 Accessed 25 September 2018, https://www.omroepzeeland.nl/nieuws/108976/Wethouder-Vlissingen-imagoschade-door-marinierscijfers and https://www.omroepzeeland.nl/nieuws/108955/Enquete-Massaal-vertrek-mariniers-bij-verhuizing-kazerne
24 Van der Schie, "Het lokale bestuur is een maatje te groot."

the so-called *superprovinces* and/or reorganize the existing twelve provinces. However, in 2014 the Rutte II administration decided that the planned superprovince of three provinces (North-Holland, Utrecht and Flevoland) to govern the Netherlands in a more efficient way and to strengthen the provincial authorities against the increasing power of the (big) cities had to stop.[25] Jouke de Vries, professor Governance and Public Policy at the Rijksuniversiteit Groningen, affirmed in an interview that the local context has become more important.[26] This seems to contradict the decision of the Rutte II administration, although it also recognizes the importance of the local context. However, 'local' can also mean the level of the city council, the provincial level, but also the national level. Depending on the context, 'local' can also mean in contradiction with the global setting. In this sense glocalization is a complex word, because it is hard to understand, as it is not always clear whether the real local, regional or national level is meant. Nevertheless, what is clear is that it contrasts with the global perspective. The same goes for regionalism, the tension between on the one hand the provinces in the Netherlands and on the other hand the regions (bigger territories of city councils). According to De Vries provinces need to work more closely together. That might be possible in a regional structure. This can become more important, because on the one hand the national administration loses tasks and authorities to Europe and on the other hand there is the development of decentralization and subsidiarity: other tasks and authorities are attributed to the regions.

For what reason is the classis on earth?
Despite the fact that scaling up does not lead automatically to reduction of costs, and that governors tend to attract more tasks and authority, the church considers that it must not miss the boat of enlargement. Geographical and mental distances are different than in the context of the Synod of Emden of 1571, the Synod of Dordrecht of 1618/1619, in the nineteenth century or even after the Second World War to give a few examples. Still, the PCN has classes, albeit smaller in number and larger in size.

The above-mentioned virtues of the *polder* can be applied to the Dutch classis. As was described above safety in the *polder* was not only important,

---

25 Accessed 25 September 2018, https://www.nu.nl/politiek/3807729/superprovincie-gaat-definitief-niet.html and https://www.nu.nl/politiek/3807191/overzicht-hindernis baan-superprovincie.html
26 Kosten, "Interview met Jouke de Vries," 6–11.

but necessary for survival. The people in the *polder* needed each other to protect themselves against the floods. This notion is absent in a theological constellation where there is no emergency requiring people to work together. The threat of disaster is absent. A local church can easily live without neighboring churches, albeit the notion of (regional) catholicity will be lost in such a case. Apparently, the more urgent the need to cooperate in order to survive, the more people are willing to form a community or entity. The classis can hardly be considered as a natural, sociological entity. They are felt as a forced constellation. This goes especially when they are scaled up.

In 1571 the Synod of Emden stated that there is no lordship of churches over one another, and also not of pastors, elders and deacons over one another: "No church, no minister, no elder, no deacon shall lord over one another, but all shall be suspect of the temptation to dominate."[27] This is echoed in section VI.1 of the church order of the PCN.[28] The office-bearers are not supposed to lord over one another, nor congregations over one another. The presbyterial-synodical system of church polity grants office-bearers in a collegial context the authority to rule the church, this includes ruling the congregants. However, this does not mean that the voice of the congregants is absent. The ecclesiological framework requires cooperation between office-bearers and congregants. Despite this golden rule there is inequality in the daily practice. As the church exists in a broken world, the visible church is imperfect.

Some consistories try to dominate or at least influence the classis (assembly) through its delegates. The existence of the *classispredikant*, the classis minister, is new in 2018. He or she is neither a bishop nor a superintendent, but is in the expression of what Klaas-Willem de Jong calls about half a bishop.[29] This office is instituted in order to serve the

---

27 In Latin: "*Nulla Ecclesia in alias, nullus minister in ministros, nullus Senior in Seniores, Diaconus en Diaconos primatum seu dominationem obtinebit, sed potius ab omni et suspitione et occasione cauebit.*" In sixteenth-century Dutch: "Gheen Kercke sal over een ander Kercke, gheen Dienaer des Woorts, gheen Ouderlinck, noch Diaken sal d'een over d'ander heerschappie voeren, maar een yeghelijck sal hen voor alle suspicien, ende aenlockinge om te heerschappen wachten;" accessed 26 September 2018, http://kerkrecht.nl/node/5945.
28 "Opdat niet het ene ambt over het andere, de ene ambtsdrager over de andere, noch de ene gemeente over de andere heerse, maar alles wordt gericht op de gehoorzaamheid aan Christus, het Hoofd van de Kerk, is de leiding in de kerk toevertrouwd aan ambtelijke vergaderingen."
29 See page 55–71.

denomination, the consistories and congregations, and the pastors, and their authority is limited in a context of checks and balances, However, this is not a guarantee that there will be no abuse of power. Apparently, for the PCN the advantages of supervision for the benefit of fellowship exceed the fear of this possible abuse. From the perspective of the former fear for supervision this seems paradoxical, but it shows that times have changed. Time will tell whether the PCN is right, and whether the denomination as a whole really benefits from the *classispredikant*. A certain or full inequality can also be present in other kind of expressions, for example the case that in some local churches women are not admitted to office, and that if they are admitted in other local congregations they are ignored by some male office-bearers in their classis.

Nonetheless, the notion of equality of the Synod of Emden does match with the virtue of just do normal within the *polder* mentality. The Dutch have difficulties with (visionary) leaders and/or authority.

Although it is not popular in the church, taking care of the material (and financial) things in the church does belong to the responsibility of the church, but such things are holy as well. It is a gift of and an assignment by the Holy Spirit. Believing also means creating order, avoiding disorder, and serving in this way God who provides order.

Within the framework of the denomination and within the structure of the classis as a geographical entity of several local churches in the neighborhood these churches do have a great deal of freedom. This was already the case in 2004 when the PCN was instituted, but due to *Kerk 2025*[30] it is even more the case. This includes the reflection about and the development of the special position of the so-called *pioniersplekken* (fresh expressions of church).[31]

Honesty was important to take together in the *polder* the responsibility for its well-being and its security. Nowadays the Dutch are well-known for being direct, albeit that this does not go for all of them. However, being direct is sometimes considered as the equivalent of being rude. This sociological context is important for the process of communication about the gospel of Jesus Christ both inside and outside the church.

---

30 See for example: accessed 18 May 2018, https://www.protestantsekerk.nl/actief-in-de-kerk/besturen/synode/generale-synode#November2016 (Kerk 2025), accessed 18 May 2018.
31 Accessed 18 May 2018, https://www.protestantsekerk.nl/actueel/agenda/agenda/vergadering-generale-synode-november-2018 (Voorproefje Mozaïek van kerken).

Although the local churches have a lot of freedom, and maybe since the implementation of *Kerk 2025* even more than before, the old notion of the Synod of Emden of 1571 that the classis is a gathering of neighboring local churches is still important and alive, or at least should be revitalized. This means that these local churches, despite their freedom, are expected to take care of each other, look after one another, and hence avoid the temptation of independentism. The classis safeguards the regional catholicity of the church, and functions in this way as a buffer between the local churches and the denomination.

Conclusion
The question in this contribution is how the classical reorganization of the PCN effects the ecclesiological and ecclesial notions of and in the 11 new classes against the backdrop of the changing societal and political context. This reorganization needs to be understood against the background of the changed societal and political context when it comes to developments like globalization, glocalization, regionalism and localism. On the one hand the PCN seems to give account of this non-ecclesial background as becomes clear from the five motives which led to the renewal project: a secular society, individual choices, a network society, digital revolution, and globalization. On the other hand the reorganization of the classis structure seems to be more the result of ecclesial than of ecclesiological reflection. Moreover, ecclesial scaling up tends to lead not only to a geographical, but far more a mental distance, let alone a spiritual distance with view to (delegated office-bearers of consistories of) other congregations and the notion of regional catholicity. The PCN tries to prevent that by including the so-called *ringen*, smaller circuits within the enlarged classes. The question whether this will really improve and assist the regional catholicity or whether it will strengthen the increasing ecclesial individualism of local churches and fresh expressions of church can only be answered in the future.

Bibliography
Beyer, Peter. "Globalization and the Institutional Modeling of Religions." In Peter Beyer and Lori Beaman, eds. *Religion, Globalization, and Culture*. Leiden/Boston: Brill, 2007, 167-187 (*International Studies in Religion and Society* 6).

Daiber, Karl-Fritz. "Die Region als sozialer und kirchlicher Handlungsraum." In Karl-Fritz Daiber and Werner Simpfendörfer, eds. *Kirche in der Region*. Stuttgart: Calwer Verlag, 1970, 15-46 (*Kirchenreform* 4).

Houkes, Annemarie. "Een gemeenschap op de rails." In Dick Kuiper and Jasper Vree, eds. *Het liep op rolletjes: De eenwording van protestant-christelijk Nederland per rail 1938-1939*. Zoetermeer: Meinema, 2007, 67-79 (*Jaarboek voor de geschiedenis van het Nederlands protestantisme na 1800* 15).

Janssen, Allan J., and Leon van den Broeke, eds. *A Collegial Bishop? The Classis and Presbytery at Issue*. Grand Rapids MI: Wm. B. Eerdmans, 2010 (*The Historical Series of the Reformed Church of America* 66).

Kosten, Mirjam. "Interview met Jouke de Vries: Ruimte voor de regio." *Groen Studie- en opinieblad van de Christenunie: Wereldwijd & lokaal* vol. 1 n°. 4 (2017), 6–11.

Kolle, Annemieke. "Van papieren gemeenschap naar direct contact: Mobiliteit en verenigingsleven tijdens de eerste decennia van het spoor." In Dick Kuiper and Jasper Vree, eds. *Het liep op rolletjes: De eenwording van protestant-christelijk Nederland per rail 1938-1939*. Zoetermeer: Meinema, 2007, 45–65 (*Jaarboek voor de geschiedenis van het Nederlands protestantisme na 1800* 15).

Kuiper, Dick, and Jasper Vree, eds. *Het liep op rolletjes: De eenwording van protestant-christelijk Nederland per rail 1938–1939*. Zoetermeer: Meinema, 2007 (*Jaarboek voor de geschiedenis van het Nederlands protestantisme na 1800* 15).

Kuiper, Dick. "'Tafel en bed was voor ons gereed': Afgescheidenen tussen anti-moderniteit en mobiliteit (1830-1870)." In Dick Kuiper and Jasper Vree, eds. *Het liep op rolletjes: De eenwording van protestant-christelijk Nederland per rail 1938-1939*. Zoetermeer: Meinema, 2007, 105–116 (*Jaarboek voor de geschiedenis van het Nederlands protestantisme na 1800* 15).

Nanini, Riccardo. "A Catholic Alternative to Globalization? The Compagnia Delle Opere." In Lionel Obadia, Donald C. Wood, eds. *The Economics of Religion: Anthropological Approaches*. Bingley UK: Emerald Group Publishing Limited, 2011, 47–76 (*Research in Economic Anthropology* 31).

Shakespeare, Steven. "A Community of the Question: Inclusive Ecclesiology." In Gerard Mannion, *Church and Religious 'Other'*. London: T&T Clark Bloomsbury Publishing, 2008, 156–167.

Sheikh, Haroon. "Tussen wereldzee en vasteland." In Van den Brink, Gabriel, ed. *Waarom is NL op aarde?: Nadenken over verleden, heden en toekomst van ons land*, Amsterdam: Boom, 2018, 211–232.

Van den Brink, Gabriel, ed. *Waarom is NL op aarde? Nadenken over verleden, heden en toekomst van ons land*, Amsterdam: Boom, 2018.

Van den Broeke, Leon. *Classis in Crisis: Om de Classicale Toekomst*. Zoetermeer: Boekencentrum, 2009.

Van den Broeke, Leon. "Non-Geographic Classes? Reformed Geography." *Journal of Reformed Theology* 7.1 (2013), 51–68.

Van den Broeke, C. [Leon], *Een geschiedenis van de classis: Classicale typen tussen idee en werkelijkheid 1571–2004*, Kampen: Kok, 2005.

Van der Schie, Patrick. "Het lokale bestuur is een maatje te groot." *Trouw*, 25 april 2016.

Van Lieburg, Fred. "Van classicale organisatie tot civil society." *Tijdschrift voor Nederlandse Kerkgeschiedenis* vol. 15 n°. 3 (september 2012), 78–83.

Digital sources
http://kerkrecht.nl/node/5945

https://www.lerenpionieren.nl/blogs-en-columns/mozaiek-van-kerkplekken/

https://www.nu.nl/politiek/3807191/overzicht-hindernisbaan-super provincie.html

https://www.nu.nl/politiek/3807729/superprovincie-gaat-definitief-niet. html

https://www.omroepzeeland.nl/nieuws/108976/Wethouder-Vlissingen-imagoschade-door-marinierscijfers

https://www.omroepzeeland.nl/nieuws/108955/Enquete-Massaal-vertrek-mariniers-bij-verhuizing-kazerne

https://www.protestantsekerk.nl/thema/kerk2025/#notakerk2025

https://www.protestantsekerk.nl/actief-in-de-kerk/besturen/synode/generale-synode#November2016 (*Kerk 2025*)

https://www.protestantsekerk.nl/actueel/agenda/agenda/vergadering-generale-synode-november-2018 (Voorproefje Mozaïek van kerken)

Half a bishop: A Critical Outline of the So-Called *Classispredikant* in the Protestant Church in the Netherlands

Klaas-Willem de Jong

"Instead of the current 74 classes, about 8 regional classes will be formed. (…) The chairman of a classis is its personal face. He or she is responsible for the congregations and ministers in his or her region and embodies the togetherness of these congregations. (…) He is not a busybody, but he has a pastoral mission. (…) The activities of the chairman, usually a minister, will be embedded in the meetings of the classis. (…) He will be elected by the regional classis (…). Together with the scribe of the general synod, the chairmen form a committee. (…) Each chairman is authorized to make decisions in conflict situations (…), but only in coordination with this board."[1] This is a summary of the first profile of the chairmen of the extended classes, which was envisioned in 2015 by the then scribe of the General Synod of the Protestant Church in the Netherlands (PCN).[2] This position is part of a renewal program, called Church 2025, intended to bring the church back to basics in the rapidly evolving, secular context of the Netherlands.[3] The general synod of the PCN unanimously decided in the same year to take the document in which this program was set forth as a starting point for further elaboration.[4] A motion to give the envisioned chairman the title of bishop was withdrawn after some discussion.[5] It was considered to be premature.[6] In one of the follow-up reports, several titles were considered: chairman of the region/classis, *pastor pastorum*, scribe of the region/classis, superintendent, deacon and minister of the region/

---

1 *Kerk 2025: Waar een Woord is*, 21–22.
2 It was the first concrete attempt to introduce a bishop-like office in the PCN and its predecessors (cf. Kronenburg, *Episcopus Oecumenicus*, 33–167; cf. also Van den Broeke, "Bishop-in-presbytery," 140–162, especially 150–159).
3 *Kerk 2025: Waar een Woord is*, 5–11.
4 *Handelingen 2015*, 233–234.
5 *Handelingen 2015*, 230–234.
6 *Handelingen 2015*, 234.

classis.⁷ Since it fits the profile best and bishop is a title used in other churches, the drafters of this document preferred the title of 'minister-bishop'.⁸ However, resistance was expected for its connotation of hierarchy, power concentrated in one person, as well as its association with apostolic succession. Therefore, the board of the synod did not propose the title of bishop. Nonetheless, about a quarter of the synod voted in favor of this title; whereas *classispredikant*, minister of the classis, was carried by a large majority.⁹ Meanwhile, the Church 2025 plans have been converted into regulations, which have come into force as of 1 May 2018. The first ministers to become *classispredikant* have been elected and called in May and June 2018.

In this contribution, I provide an outline of this new position in the PCN. Subsequently, I discuss recent theology within the PCN which revaluates the bishop, including some recent developments that give rise to a bishop-like office. Further, I examine the office of the moderator in the United Reformed Church (URC) in the United Kingdom. I picked the URC, because its ecclesiastical structure and its theological convictions – also in its diversity – resemble that of the PCN. The subtle differences between the moderator and the *classispredikant* help to sharpen the view on the *classispredikant*. Finally, I evaluate this new position in the PCN and formulate an answer to my research question to what extent the *classispredikant* can be called a bishop.

The rehabilitation of the bishop in recent Reformed theology in the Netherlands

There always have been episcopal elements in the organization of the Dutch churches of the reformation.¹⁰ Hans Kronenburg relates them to the ordained ministers.¹¹ Others, like Leon van den Broeke, point particularly to the classis/presbytery.¹² Apart from some individual

---

7 *Kerk 2025: Een stap verder*, 15–17.
8 *Kerk 2025: Een stap verder*, 17.
9 *Handelingen 2016*, 60. Unfortunately, the minutes of the synod have not yet been published.
10 Kronenburg, *Episcopus*, 39–167.
11 The administration of Word and sacrament is restricted to the ordained minister; only an ordained minister has the authority to ordain; some ministers of the classis are appointed to visit the congregations (Kronenburg, *Episcopus*, 61–66).
12 Van den Broeke, "The Protestant Classis: Between Episcopè and Koinonia," 75–91. Cf. in the same volume Janssen, "The Classis/Presbytery as an Expression of the Apostolicity of the Church", 63–74.

opinions from the 1930s onwards, the call for a bishop-like office grew, especially among theologians.[13] Yet, it was only after the Lima report *Baptism, Eucharist and Ministry* (BEM, 1982) that this call became substantial.[14] Three PhD studies, defended in 2000 and 2003, mark the broader acceptance of the idea on a theological level. The first study dates back to 2000 and reflects directly on the Lima report.[15] The author, Eddy van der Borght, evaluates the Reformed theology of ministry in the light of this ecumenical document. He is convinced the reformers rejected the bishop out of fear of misuse of power. He himself sees a bishop as a presbyter, a servant of the Word 'not at the local level like the minister, but at the level beyond the local one'. His 'task has a strong liturgical and pastoral content. (…) In this way, he can become a symbol of unity in the church'.[16] Margriet Gosker defended the same theme in her dissertation a few weeks earlier in the very same year. She emphasizes the underlying principle that minister and bishop share the same office.[17] Nevertheless, unlike Van der Borght she hardly expresses herself about the tasks the bishop should undertake.

In 2003, Hans Kronenburg elaborated these insights into a theology of the bishop. He discerns four motives to support the introduction of an episcopal ministry: a pastoral motive (response to the need for 'leadership with a human face'), an ecclesiological motive (a bridge 'between unity and pluriformity', local and national church, authority and management), an ecumenical motive and a cultural (or missionary) motive.[18] Using the method *lex orandi, lex credendi,* Kronenburg analyzes four rites for the ordination of a bishop to develop a profile of a bishop. In his view, a bishop has the following characteristics. He or she is to be elected by the community, does not work without other office-bearers and is committed to the authority of a synod.[19] He serves 'as *pastor pastorum* (a), as commissioner of those who are sent out (*apostolos*) (b), as teacher and guardian of the tradition of the faith (c), as a sign of unity and as a president of the liturgy (d), as a link between the local and the universal church (e), as the voice

---

13 Kronenburg, *Episcopus*, 77–167.
14 Cf. *Baptism, Eucharist and Ministry* (= *BEM*).
15 Van der Borght, *Het ambt her-dacht*. I cite the English version: Van der Borght, *Theology of Ministry*.
16 Quotes in both this sentence and the sentence before: Van der Borght, *Theology of Ministry*, 433.
17 Gosker, *Het ambt in de oecumenische discussie*, 238f, 362.
18 Kronenburg, *Episcopus*, 225–240, 498.
19 Kronenburg, *Episcopus*, 500 (cf. 469, 476).

of conscience (f), and as ordainer (g)'.[20] Kronenburg sees aspect d as the heart of the profile, whereas the aspects a and g, b and f, as well as c and e are closely related: "In all his words and actions, a bishop is accountable for (…) his integrity (…) his spirituality and (…) his willingness to serve".[21]

As I will later compare the outcome of Kronenburg's research to the profile of the *classispredikant* in the PCN, I would first like to note a few concerns I have about his work. The first of these involves the method *lex orandi, lex credendi* as such. Kronenburg values the liturgy as normative, although he admits there should be an interplay between liturgy and doctrine.[22] In this case, however, I doubt whether the liturgy has a value of its own. Kronenburg analyzes four relatively recent ordination rites, each of which in my opinion must be considered a well-conceived result of an ecclesiastical process.[23] Kronenburg does not clearly explain what exactly the liturgy adds to the already existing lived doctrine. On the contrary, I believe all he reveals about the profile of a bishop can be found in doctrinal texts too. Secondly, I am concerned about the way Kronenburg applies the method. Kronenburg favorably refers to Geoffrey Wainwright, but he neglects to use the fundamental rules Wainwright sets out, nor does he elaborate the method himself.[24] Furthermore, it is unclear how Kronenburg determines what parts of the different liturgies are more valuable than others. What seems to be decisive is whether something fits his image of the early Christian tradition or not. Thus, the result of Kronenburg's thorough examination of the ordination texts is more or less a sum of the various tasks he discovers studying these rites. Note, moreover, that the first two characteristics he mentions are the same as two out of the three 'Guiding Principles for the Exercise of the Ordained Ministry' in the BEM report, which have been applied to the bishop.[25] The tasks in the heart of Kronenburg's profile can be traced back to only a small section of the rite (i.e. the introduction into the examination),

---

20 Kronenburg, *Episcopus*, 500 (cf. 469, 476), but cf. also 381.
21 Kronenburg, *Episcopus*, 500 (cf. 469, 476).
22 Kronenburg, *Episcopus*, 276–82.
23 Kronenburg, *Episcopus*, 282–299 (303).
24 Cf. Wainwright, *Doxology*, 242–250 (especially 243–45) who suggests "three kinds of test – those of origin, of spread, and of ethical correspondence – that help to determine when worship (…) can in fact properly be drawn on as a doctrinal source (245). Cf. also Kay, "The Lex orandi in recent Protestant Theology," 11–23, especially 21.
25 Cf. *BEM*, 23 (n°. 26), cf. Kronenburg, *Episcopus*, 169f.

which is basically of a doctrinal character itself.[26] It is not surprising that almost all tasks can be found in the BEM report as well.[27] Finally, the last three elements of the profile concerning the accountability of the bishop revolve around another small section of the ordination rites, namely the examination.[28] Despite these concerns, I will use Kronenburg's profile because it reflects the essentials mentioned in the BEM report and it is the only detailed and well-substantiated profile tailored to the Dutch protestant context.

The practical need for a bishop-like office or officer
Besides the principal and theological considerations, there are several developments in the PCN which give rise to the need for an office such as the PCN outlined in its Church 2025. The first development is primarily internal. Like many denominations in Western Europe, the PCN is in decline. The same amount of work has to be done by fewer people. It can be especially difficult to complete tasks at a level beyond the local. I want to mention two implications of this development in particular. First, it was difficult to find delegates for the meetings of the classes.[29] Some of these meetings rarely reached a quorum. This was an important reason behind the decision to drastically diminish the number of classes from 74 to initially 8; in the end, the number decided on was 11.[30] Second, it became nearly impossible to find sufficient suitable office-bearers for a specialized and labor-intensive task such as the regular visitation of the congregations.[31] Hence, there was a shortage in both quantity and quality.

The second development I want to point out, in conjunction with the latter aspect, is the waning interest in the regular visitation especially among the congregations. The congregations sometimes experienced it as disappointing or even unnecessary and useless. The meaning of this kind of visitation had become unclear to them. It needed to be improved in form as well as in content.[32] Originally, in the project Church 2025 a

---

26 Cf. Kronenburg, *Episcopus*, 367–382. Because the rite of the Church of South India omits such an introduction, Kronenburg chooses to consult the doctrine in that case (368). Kronenburg is less explicit in the description of the relationship between the other aspects of the profile and the examined ordination rites.
27 Cf. *BEM*, 24 (n°. 29).
28 Kronenburg, *Episcopus*, 382–399.
29 *Kerk 2025: Waar een Woord is*, 21.
30 *Kerk 2025: Een stap verder*, 10f.
31 *Kerk 2025: Waar een Woord is*, 23.
32 *Kerk 2025: Waar een Woord is*, 23.

less frequent and more qualified visit of the congregations by the chairman and one of the members of the visitation board was foreseen.[33] In a later stage, this task was considered to be more suitable for the *classispredikant*, as a part of his pastoral mission.[34] The visitation board got another responsibility. Until the plans of Church 2025 were implemented, congregations met in both visitation and in the classis meetings. In the new constellation, the board is commissioned to facilitate the encounter between the congregations in other ways.[35]

Thirdly, since the beginning of the 1960s, in the two largest predecessors of the PCN, there has been an ongoing reflection on the pastoral support of ministers.[36] In the Netherlands Reformed Church, the observation that hundreds of ministers felt the need to move to another congregation because of a mismatch with their present congregation, was the initial reason for this reflection.[37] In the Reformed Churches in the Netherlands, the scope was broader from the outset. They basically investigated the need for pastoral care among and for ministers.[38] However, the *pastor pastorum* was not introduced in these denominations. In the smallest predecessor of the PCN, the Evangelical-Lutheran Church, the chairman of the synod, called president, had the duty to appoint one or more ministers as *pastor pastorum*. They functioned on his behalf.[39] The function of *pastor pastorum* ceased to exist when the three churches merged into the PCN in 2004. In 2012 the general synod of the PCN turned down a new proposal to introduce a *pastor pastorum*.[40] It established there was no need for such a figure; ministers and pastoral workers could approach others for pastoral care. Moreover, according to the synod, a *pastor pastorum* might imply a certain hierarchy. Yet, in the context of Church 2025, the subject came up again. Pastoral care was considered necessary for ministers in their often demanding and insecure

---

33 *Kerk 2025: Waar een Woord is*, 23.
34 *Kerk 2025: Een stap verder*, 8.
35 *Kerk 2025: Een stap verder*, 8f; cf. *Kerk 2025, Waar een Woord is*, 22.
36 Apart from the visitation in which always separate attention was paid to the ministers.
37 Kronenburg, *Episcopus*, 136–138.
38 Kronenburg, *Episcopus*, 151–153.
39 *Ordeningen voor de Evangelisch-Lutherse Kerk in het Koninkrijk der Nederlanden*, X Ordening op het pastoraat over het openbare ambt.
40 *Handelingen 2012* (Utrecht: Protestantse Kerk in Nederland, 2014), 324f. Cf. "Pastor Pastorum. Rapport van de Beleidscommissie Predikanten. KT 12-10," PCN, accessed July 27, 2018, https://www.protestantsekerk.nl/download/CAwdEAwUUkNCX0A=&inline=0

position.⁴¹ Still, in the Church 2025 project this care was made concrete only as a part of measures to improve the mobility of the ministers. Therefore, according to the first Church 2025 report a *classispredikant*, acting as *pastor pastorum*, shall raise the issue of mobility in the meetings with the ministers in his district at regular times.⁴²

The fourth development I want to highlight is a direct result of the decreasing popularity of churches. The PCN increasingly faces missionary challenges. The *classispredikant* represents the church in a certain region or province. He or she provides a personal face for the PCN on site, making it more recognizable and approachable.⁴³

Fifthly, the traditional way of dealing with conflict and discipline situations proved to be inadequate. Because of the various boards involved, it is slow-moving and laborious process. It is expected that an officer such as the *classispredikant*, having effective powers of intervention in certain situations and subject to certain conditions, would be able to deal with these situations in an earlier stage and generally more effectively.⁴⁴ This is supported by the impression that there is a growing demand for personal authority in both church and society.⁴⁵ One could argue that the consolidation to approximately ten classes and consequently most of the restructuring at the level of the classis was not only due to shortages of personal resources, but was also meant to financially enable the introduction of a position like the *classispredikant* in order to establish stronger leadership in the PCN.

Taking the foregoing into account, it seems that the enlargement of the classes and the introduction of the *classispredikant* offer considerable benefits. However, there is an important side effect as well which has been acknowledged increasingly during the reorganization process. In the PCN, the classis is not only the most obvious ecclesiastical body for *episkopē*, but for *koinōnia* too.⁴⁶ Until 1 May 2018, PCN congregations came together – or were supposed to come together – in the classes. As classes have been enlarged and not every congregation retains a delegate

---

41 *Kerk 2025: Waar*, 27f. Cf. *Kerk 2025: Een stap*, 7f. However, cf. also relativizing remarks with regard to ministers: "Apart from pastoral workers (…) *also* (…) ministers will serve the church in the coming period" (emphasis added) and "However, only raising concerns would conjure up the wrong image." (*Kerk 2025: Waar*, 27f)
42 *Kerk 2025: Waar een Woord is*, 29.
43 *Kerk 2025: Waar een Woord is*, 21.
44 *Kerk 2025: Waar een Woord is*, 22f.
45 *Kerk 2025: Waar een Woord is*, 23.
46 Cf. Van den Broeke, "The Protestant Classis," 79, 80f, 87f.

in the newly established classis, this opportunity to meet no longer exists for all congregations. Therefore, a new platform has been created where congregations can meet, the so-called *ring*, a regional encounter.[47] This platform has no authority and has been placed under the responsibility of the visitation board of the classis, in particular of its chairman. On the one hand, the task of the visitation board has been reduced: the *classispredikant* has taken over the regular visitation. On the other hand, its responsibilities have been broadened: it also has to take care of the encounter between congregations. The *classispredikant* and the chairman of the visitation board are supposed to cooperate closely.[48] The chairman is a member of the board of the classis, but he only has an advisory role.[49]

Theological motives
Thus far in this contribution, I have set out the motives behind the introduction of the *classispredikant*. With exception of the representative task, the responsibilities ascribed to him or her not only belonged to the responsibilities of the classis but remain, for the function of the *classispredikant* is principally embedded in the classis. These responsibilities have been shown to be largely of a practical and functional nature. In the initial document of Church 2025, they have been substantiated theologically in a constrained way, only referring to the unity in Christ and the embodiment of this unity in a person rather than in a board.[50] In fact, a sounder theological basis was laid afterwards in a follow-up report, using the story of Barnabas – visiting the congregation of Antiochia, counseling it and encouraging it to remain faithful – and explicitly referring to the unity in Christ, the catholicity of the church and the episcopal role of both classis and *classispredikant*.[51] Some of these aspects are also processed into the official job description of the *classispredikant*.[52]

---

47 "Kerk 2025. Deel 1: Classes en kerkelijke presentie. Toelichting op het voorstel voor de tweede lezing," accessed July 31, 2018, https://www.protestantsekerk.nl/download/CAwdEAwUUkRHXkk=&type=pdf (6-9); *Kerk 2025: Waar een Woord is*, 22; *Kerk 2025: Een stap verder*, 5, 8–9.
48 E.g. *Kerk 2025: Een stap verder*, 9; "Kerk 2025. Deel 1," 23f.
49 *Kerk 2025: Waar een Woord is*, 22, 23; *Kerk 2025: Een stap verder*, 9; "Kerk 2025. Deel 1," 26f.
50 *Kerk 2025: Waar een Woord is*, 16, 23.
51 *Kerk 2025: Een stap verder*, 7f.
52 "Profiel, functieomschrijving en benoeming van de classispredikant – versie 5," accessed 1 August, 2018, https://www.protestantsekerk.nl/download/CAwdEAwUUkZKW0A=&type=pdf

Comparison with the moderator in the URC
The *classispredikant* resembles the office of the moderator of the URC in the United Kingdom, although there are resemblances to moderators in other churches as well.[53] The moderator functions at the same regional level as the *classispredikant*, which is called a synod in the URC. A covenant between the URC and several other denominations in the early 1980s implied that the URC moderator, as it was, was not acknowledged as a bishop because of the absence of apostolic succession, apparently at least not by the Church of England at that time.[54]

Hereafter I will discuss the main provisions in the URC Manual regarding a moderator and compare them with the regulations in the recently revised PCN church order. I do so to get a sharper image of the *classispredikant* and the choices made in the designing of his profile.

In both churches there is no indication of the office or function in the founding legislation.[55] Furthermore, it is noteworthy that the provisions for the moderator are literally embedded in the rulings of the regional synod. The moderator functions within the frameworks of the synod; he is a part of it, just as the *classispredikant* is meant to be in the PCN.

At the heart of the tasks of both moderator and *classispredikant* is the commission to execute a pastoral office towards ministers and congregations.[56] It seems logical therefore that in both churches the office-bearer must be a minister. This minister shall, in the words of the URC, 'be separated from any local pastoral charge'.[57] Initially, in the PCN it seemed that it was not absolutely necessary for the *classispredikant* to be an

---

53 Cf. "The Manual. Section B: The Structure of the United Reformed Church," accessed July 31, 2018, https://www.urc.org.uk/images/the_manual/B_The_structure_of_the_URC_18_10_17.pdf (6). Cf. e.g. "Office of the Moderator of the General Assembly Regulations," accessed July 31, 2018, http://www.churchofscotland.org.uk/__data/assets/pdf_file/0004/14836/2013-reg-2-Duties-of-the-Moderator.pdf (Church of Scotland). Note these regulations are meant for a moderator at a national level.
54 Cf. Camroux, *Ecumenism in Retreat*.
55 PCN: "Kerkorde en Ordinanties van de Protestantse Kerk in Nederland versie mei 2018," accessed July 31, 2018, https://www.protestantsekerk.nl/download/CAwdEAwUUkVGVkE=&inline=0 (esp. 3–11); URC: "The Manual. Section A: The Basis of the Union," accessed July 31, 2018, https://www.urc.org.uk/images/the_manual/A_The_Basis_of_union_18_10_17.pdf (especially 1-8).
56 PCN: *Kerk 2025: Waar een Woord is*, 21; *Kerk 2025: Een stap verder*, 7f; "Kerkorde," 45 (ord. 4-16-3); URC: "The Manual. Section B," 6.
57 "The Manual. Section B," 6. Cf. *Kerk 2025: Waar een Woord is*, 21, 23; *Kerk 2025, Een stap verder*, 9f. The wording in the URC Manual is principled, whereas it is in the PCN more practical.

ordained minister; in a later stage of the project, however, it was made clear that this would indeed be necessary.[58] As a minister, he fits the bishop-like profile the abovementioned theologians created. Furthermore, in both churches the officers meet with their colleagues regularly.[59] Yet, in other respects the descriptions of moderator and *classispredikant* differ subtly.

While the moderator is appointed by the URC general assembly, in the PCN it is the classis itself which elects the *classispredikant* after it has consulted the general synod.[60] In my opinion, the election and appointment by another authority than the classis can strengthen the independent position of a *classispredikant*. However, he would then lack a solid basis in both the classis which he serves and the congregations belonging to the classis. Moreover, in the reorganization process of Church 2025 a considerable number of congregations expressed the opinion that the diminishing of the number of classis, and thus the enlarging of each classis, increases the distance between the local basis of the church and the assemblies at a regional and a national level.[61] Therefore, from a tactical point of view it would not have been wise to introduce a *classispredikant* elected by the general synod. In the recent regulations of the PCN in which the *classispredikant* is embedded, he cannot even be elected into the general synod and represent the classis there as a delegate.[62]

---

58 Cf. *Kerk 2025: Waar een Woord is*, 21, and *Kerk 2025: Een stap verder*, 10. In the before also mentioned Church of Scotland it also may be a deacon or and elder ("Church Courts Act (Act III 2000)," accessed 31 July, 2018, http://www.churchofscotland.org.uk/__data/assets/pdf_file/0005/45734/2000_Act_3_Church_Courts_consolidating_act_from_1_January_2018.pdf (art. 7 (a)).

59 PCN: *Kerk 2025: Waar een Woord is*, 22; *Kerk 2025: Een stap verder*, 9; there is no provision referring to this meeting in the "Kerkorde"; URC: "The Manual. Section B," 6.

60 URC: "The Manual. Section B," 6, 13; PCN: *Kerk 2025: Waar*, 21; *Kerk 2025: Een stap*, 10; "Kerkorde," 45 (ord. 4-16-2). Though the board of the general synod, in my opinion, only had a limited authority according to the prevailing church order, it heavily influenced the election of the *classispredikanten* in May and June 2018 (see my blog "Landelijke bemoeienis op regionaal niveau – de classispredikant," accessed 31 July 2018, http://blog.kerkenrecht.nl/2018/05/21/landelijke-bemoeienis-op-regionaal-niveau-de-classispredikant/

61 Cf. "Kerk 2025. Deel 1," 3f.

62 "Kerkorde," 49 (ord. 4–24–3).

Next, a task of the moderator is to 'preside over the meetings of the synod'.[63] Initially, this was also the case in the PCN.[64] At a later stage, there were objections regarding the large range of tasks of the *classispredikant*, including his chairmanship. The major objection, however, was that the *classispredikant* may make certain decisions on his own in urgent situations, but in all cases these decisions need to be subsequently confirmed by the board of the classis.[65] Moreover, he has to be accountable in full classis meetings for the decisions he has made in the preceding period.[66] If the *classispredikant* serves as the chairman of these meetings, it may be difficult to ensure his accountability. In the URC, the moderator lacks this kind of power and accountability to his own synod, for he is elected by the general synod.

Furthermore, attention should be drawn to the additional support a *classispredikant* can call upon when executing his major, pastoral mission. As I mentioned above, every classis must appoint a board for the visitation. In the initial plans the *classispredikant* was empowered to summon this board to execute an extraordinary visitation in conflict situations and to give him its advisory opinion.[67] In a later, definite phase, the proposals were weakened and each of them became its own responsibility. The *classispredikant* is explicitly allowed to ask for an extraordinary visitation, but the visitation board itself makes the decision.[68] On the other hand, if the board is of the opinion that a visitation shall be executed, it has to consult the *classispredikant* first.[69] On the basis of the visitation report, though, it is the board of the classis which must decide whether measures should be taken, taking the advice of the chairman of the visitation board into account.[70]

---

63 URC: "The Manual. Section B," 6.
64 *Kerk 2025: Waar een Woord is*, 22; *Kerk 2025: Een stap verder*, 9
65 "Kerk 2025. Deel 1: (…) tweede lezing," 4f. In *Kerk 2025: Waar een Woord is*, 22, this authority is worded in a essentially different way: the classispredikant only can take a decision "in consultation with" the board of the classis (so, confirmation beforehand is needed). The context shows this must be due to sloppiness.
66 "Kerkorde," 45 (ord. 4–16–7, cf. 4–15–8); cf. in general terms *Kerk 2025: Waar een Woord is*, 21f; *Kerk 2025: Een stap verder*, 8.
67 *Kerk 2025: Waar een Woord is*, 22f; *Kerk 2025: Een stap verder*, 8f.
68 "Kerkorde," 45 (ord. 4–16–4).
69 "Kerkorde," 65 (ord. 10–5–2).
70 "Kerkorde," 45 (ord. 4–16–4). Strictly speaking, the chairman of the visitation board only has a right to advice when the classispredikant has asked for an extraordinary visitation.

However, the moderator in the URC too has a few competences that the *classispredikant* does not.[71] He fulfills the responsibility ascribed to him under the URC Disciplinary Process and the Incapacity Procedure. In both procedures he conducts a leading role in the preliminary phase.[72] For example, under certain conditions he himself may suspend the minister concerned.[73] Apart from these far-reaching executive powers, he nominates potential candidates for vacant pastorates and presides at ordinations and/or inductions or appoints a deputy to preside. All these tasks are in line with his pastoral office, but also refer to the episcopal task of ordaining ministers. They empower him to effectively influence the ecclesiastical life in his region. In this respect, the competences of the *classispredikant* are very limited, even in his task to promote the mobility of ministers. He can only use his personal influence. As far as I can see, the role of the URC moderator in the Disciplinary Process and the Incapacity Procedure in the preparatory stage of proceedings is more profound than the power of the *classispredikant* to intervene. On the other hand, the power invested in the *classispredikant* is not confined to disciplinary proceedings but covers measures which can be used in a broader variety of cases.[74] In my opinion, in both denominations it is questionable to what extent one can confide in the *pastor pastorum*. What one says in confidence at one moment can be used against him at another.[75]

Finally, from a missionary point of view, it is important to note the authority to speak on behalf of the classis outside the PCN – 'in contacts with other denominations, civil society organizations, governments and media within its jurisdiction' – has been put into words explicitly in the PCN.[76] In the URC the moderator lacks such an authority, though, it is

---

71 Cf. "The Manual. Section B," 6.
72 "The Manual. Section O: The Ministerial Disciplinary Process," accessed July 31, 2018, https://urc.org.uk/images/the_manual/O_Ministerial_disciplinary_process.pdf; "The Manual. Section P: Procedure for dealing with cases of incapacity involving ministers or church-related community workers," accessed 31 July, 2018, https://urc.org.uk/images/the_manual/IP_from_March_2016.pdf.
73 "The Manual. Section O," B.7.1ff, E; "The Manual. Section P," B.1.2ff.
74 In fact, in urgent cases he is entitled to take all measures the board of the classis is entitled to take ("Kerkorde," 45 (ord. 4–16–5)).
75 Perhaps a solution can be found outside the office of the *classispredikant* in the appointment of an independent counselor for the pastorate regarding ministers.
76 "Kerkorde," 45 (ord. 4–16–6).

not excluded completely. He shall 'stimulate and encourage the work of the URC within the province or nation'.[77]

In conclusion, it appears that in comparison with the moderator the *classispredikant* has a less independent position and has less authority. This may be explained by the fear of misuse of power Van der Borght perceives in Reformed theology, in particular in the Netherlands.

Conclusion
The motives behind the introduction of a bishop identified by Hans Kronenburg can be recognized in the ideals of the Church 2025 project and the rules connected with them. To determine whether the *classispredikant* can be considered a bishop, I look at whether the position meets the criteria established by Kronenburg.

From the fact that the *classispredikant* is not mentioned in the founding legislation of the PCN, I deduce this office is not crucial for the organization of the PCN, in any case not from a theological point of view. The introduction of the *classispredikant* serves mainly practical purposes. Still, this does not exclude the implicit application of underlying theological principles.

The framework for the *classispredikant* is the framework Kronenburg outlines: elected by the community (in this case, the classis), working with other office-bearers, and committed to the authority of a synod (again, in this case, the classis).

According to Kronenburg, a bishop should be a sign of unity. This key notion is found in several underlying documents of the Church 2025 project, but this aspect is only scarcely included in the final, practically phrased regulations: the *classispredikant* embodies the responsibility of the classis to supervise – as part of the *episkopē* – congregations and office-bearers.[78] However, this does not compel the *classispredikant* to restrain himself from behaving as a bishop and being observed as such.

The same applies for most of the other characteristics. Admittedly, the *classispredikant* is officially encouraged to serve as a pastor for both congregations and office-bearers, but he is not explicitly encouraged to witness publicly, to stimulate missionary activities, to teach and guard the tradition of faith, or to link the local and universal church. However, he is not forbidden from engaging in these activities either. On the contrary, outside the PCN he is given the opportunity to speak on behalf of the

---

77 URC: "The Manual. Section B," 6.
78 "Kerkorde," 45 (ord. 4–16–1), cf. 9 (art. XII–4) and 43 (ord. 4–14–1).

classis. I expect a charismatic *classispredikant* will in practice be able to fulfill almost all requirements.

Only one of Kronenburg's characteristics is missing completely, namely the ordainer. References to this, such as can be seen in the URC, are completely absent. The *classispredikant* will not be ordained in apostolic succession, nor has he himself the exclusive authority to ordain others, let alone to ordain others in this succession.[79] Hence, probably most episcopal churches will not acknowledge him as a bishop. Nevertheless, provisions as in the URC to propose candidates for vacancies and to be present (or to be represented) at ordinations and inductions, could be inserted easily in the prevailing church order. If the PCN strives for a more bishop-like office or officer, it could consider taking over such regulations and/or introducing concrete regulations to promote the mobility of ministers.

Despite the acknowledgment by other denominations of the *classispredikant* as a bishop, according to the current PCN regulations he is at most half a bishop; however, he does have the potential to develop into an almost whole one.

Bibliography

Baptism, Eucharist and Ministry (= *BEM*). Geneva: World Council of Churches, 1982.

Camroux, Martin. *Ecumenism in Retreat: How the United Reformed Church Failed to Break the Mould*. Eugene OR: Wipf & Stock, 2016.

Gosker, Margriet. *Het ambt in de oecumenische discussie: De betekenis van de Lima-ambtstekst*. Delft: Eburon, 2000.

Handelingen 2012. Utrecht: Protestantse Kerk in Nederland, 2014.

Handelingen 2015. Utrecht: Protestantse Kerk in Nederland, 2016.

Handelingen 2016. Utrecht: Protestantse Kerk in Nederland, 2019.

---

79 Cf. also Gosker, *Het ambt*, 240 (cf. 362), Van der Borght, *Theology*, 295–338 and 421–423).

Janssen, Allan J. "The Classis/Presbytery as an Expression of the Apostolicity of the Church." In *A Collegial Bishop? Classis and Presbytery at Issue*, Allan J. Janssen and Leon van den Broeke, eds. Grand Rapids MI: Eerdmans, 2010, 63–74.

Kay, J.F. "The Lex orandi in recent Protestant Theology." In *Ecumenical Theology in Worship, Doctrine, and Life: Essays Presented to Geoffrey Wainwright on his Sixtieth Birthday*. David S. Cunningham, Ralph Del Colle, Lucas Lamadrid, eds. New York: Oxford University Press, 2000, 11–23.

Kerk 2025: Waar een Woord is, is een weg. Utrecht: Protestantse Kerk in Nederland, (January) 2016.

Kerk 2025: Een stap verder. Utrecht, Protestantse Kerk in Nederland, (April) 2016.

Kronenburg, J. *Episcopus Oecumenicus: Bouwstenen voor een theologie van het bisschopsambt in een verenigde reformatorische kerk*. Zoetermeer: Meinema, 2003.

Ordeningen voor de Evangelisch-Lutherse Kerk in het Koninkrijk der Nederlanden, X Ordening op het pastoraat over het openbare ambt.

Van den Broeke, C. [Leon]. "*Bishop-in-presbytery:* De classicale bisschop?" *NTKR: Tijdschrift voor Recht en Religie* 5 (2011), 140–162.

Van den Broeke, Leon. "The Protestant Classis: Between Episcopè and Koinonia." In *A Collegial Bishop? Classis and Presbytery at Issue*. Allan J. Janssen and Leon van den Broeke, eds. Grand Rapids MI: Eerdmans, 2010, 75–91.

Van der Borght, E.A.J.G. *Het ambt her-dacht: De gereformeerde ambtstheologie in het licht van het rapport Baptism, Eucharist and Ministry (Lima, 1982) van de theologische commissie van Faith and Order van de Wereldraad van Kerken*. Zoetermeer: Meinema, 2000.

Van der Borght, Eduardus. *Theology of Ministry: A Reformed Contribution to an Ecumenical Dialogue*. Leiden: Brill, 2007.

Wainwright, Geoffrey. *Doxology: The praise of God in Worship, Doctrine and Liefe. A Systematic Theology*. London: Epworth Press, 1980, 242–250.

Digital sources

"Church Courts Act (Act III 2000)," http://www.churchofscotland.org.uk/__data/assets/pdf_file/0005/45734/2000_Act_3_Church_Courts_consolidating_act_from_1_January_2018.pdf (art. 7 (a)).

"Kerk 2025. Deel 1: Classes en kerkelijke presentie. Toelichting op het voorstel voor de tweede lezing," https://www.protestantsekerk.nl/download/CAwdEAwUUkRHXkk=&type=pdf (p. 6–9).

"Kerkorde en Ordinanties van de Protestantse Kerk in Nederland versie mei 2018," https://www.protestantsekerk.nl/download/CAwdEAwUUkVGVkE=&inline=0 (esp. p. 3–11).

"Landelijke bemoeienis op regionaal niveau – de classispredikant," http://blog.kerkenrecht.nl/2018/05/21/landelijke-bemoeienis-op-regionaal-niveau-de-classispredikant/

"The Manual. Section A: The Basis of the Union," https://www.urc.org.uk/images/the_manual/A_The_Basis_of_union_18_10_17.pdf (esp. 1–8).

"The Manual. Section B: The Structure of the United Reformed Church," https://www.urc.org.uk/images/the_manual/B_The_structure_of_the_URC_18_10_17.pdf (6).

"The Manual. Section O: The Ministerial Disciplinary Process," https://urc.org.uk/images/the_manual/O_Ministerial_disciplinary_process.pdf.

"The Manual. Section P: Procedure for dealing with cases of incapacity involving ministers or church-related community workers," https://urc.org.uk/images/the_manual/IP_from_March_2016.pdf.

"Office of the Moderator of the General Assembly Regulations," http://www.churchofscotland.org.uk/__data/assets/pdf_file/0004/14836/2013-reg-2-Duties-of-the-Moderator.pdf (Church of Scotland).

"Pastor Pastorum. Rapport van de Beleidscommissie Predikanten. KT 12-10," PCN, https://www.protestantsekerk.nl/download/CAwdEAwUUkNCX0A=&inline=0.

"Profiel, functieomschrijving en benoeming van de classispredikant – versie 5," https://www.protestantsekerk.nl/download/CAwdEAwUUkZKW0A=&type=pdf.

Balancing Tensions and Encouraging Health: The Classis Renewal Movement in the Christian Reformed Church in North America

Kathleen S. Smith

Introduction
Ten years ago, a conference was held at the New Brunswick Theological Seminary in New Jersey, U.S.A., on "A Collegial Bishop? Classis and Presbytery at Issue." Following the conference, a book was published containing the conference presentations, and in that book, Leon van den Broeke identified two different understandings of the classis in his chapter, "Between Episcopè and Koinonia."[1] He wrote of the difference between an understanding of the classis as providing oversight and functioning as a bishop, contrasted with a newer understanding of the classis as a place for sharing, relationships, and community.

These two different understandings of the classis – *episkopē* and *koinōnia* – are also operative in the Christian Reformed Church in North America (CRCNA). In fact, in 2018, many classes in the CRCNA are leaning in the direction of the newer understanding of the classis as *koinōnia*, and this has resulted in a need to balance the tensions between these two understandings in this denomination.

This essay will describe how the classis functions in the CRCNA, what the historic and currently changing ecclesiastical vision for the classis is in this North American denomination, and how that vision relates to the leadership of the denomination. It will also describe how the CRCNA is balancing the tensions between different understandings of the classis, while also encouraging health and growth in its churches and classes.

The function of the classis in the CRCNA
Throughout its history, the CRCNA has understood the classis as a gathering of delegates from the churches in a geographical region, an understanding inherited from the Synod of Dordt of 1618-1619. These

---
1 Janssen/Van den Broeke, *A Collegial Bishop?*, 75–91.

delegates assemble to do the business of the church – to perform the episcopal function, as identified by Van den Broeke. They consider various matters for approval, such as the candidates for ministry; the organization, merging, and dissolution of churches; various ministerial credentialing matters; and disciplinary matters related to church members and office-bearers. In this understanding of the classis as an assembly, the classis only exists when it is in session.

In the CRCNA, the classis has been defined by its Church Order's Article 39: "A classis shall consist of a group of neighboring churches," and by Article 40: "The council of each church shall delegate a minister, and elder, and a deacon to the classis."[2] Except for the addition of the delegation of deacons to the classis in 2015, this is very much a reflection of the DCO in its Article 41: "The classical meetings shall consist of neighboring churches, each of which shall delegate with proper credentials one minister and one elder to the meeting of classis."[3]

The CRCNA's Church Order Article 39 goes on to say: "The organizing of a new classis and the redistricting of classes require the approval of synod."[4] This 'redistricting' includes the transfer of churches from one classis to another. A Supplement to Article 39 was added by Synod 1996 that gives the reasons for such transfers. It said, "Any request for transfer to another classis may include grounds that go beyond the sole matter of geographic proximity; synod is at liberty to consider such grounds in its disposition of the request."[5] This addition was made during the years of debates regarding women in ecclesiastical office in the CRCNA, and came soon after Synod 1995 had allowed women to be ordained to the offices of minister, elder, and evangelist by way of exception at the classical level.[6] At that time, the Church Order retained the requirement that such offices be filled only by male confessing members.

The geographic understanding of the classis had thus been challenged by those who were seeking theological affinity, but that affinity was directly related to their positions on issues such as women in ecclesiastical office. While this matter is a theological issue and an issue of biblical

---

2 *Church Order and its Supplements 2018*, 82–83.
3 Hall/Hall, *Paradigms in Polity*, 180.
4 *Church Order and its Supplements 2018*, 82.
5 *Acts of Synod 1996*, 561.
6 *Acts of Synod 1995*, 733.

interpretation, in the CRCNA it has been treated as a church order issue and has been dealt with at the classis level. In 1995, synod allowed classes to take exception to the male requirement for the offices of minister, elder, and evangelist,[7] and to ordain women to those offices. In 2007, that male requirement was removed from the Church Order, but synod allowed classes to take an exception in a different way. Those who did not support the ordination of women were allowed to follow their convictions by not seating women delegates at their classis meetings.[8] In 2007, just under half of the 48 classes did not allow women to be seated, but today the trend is toward more openness, with only four classes still not allowing women delegates to their classis meetings.[9]

Churches requesting transfers from one classis to another in recent years have sometimes given the rationale of geographical and distance issues, but some were also related to the issue of women in ecclesiastical office. For instance, three requests for transfer came to Synod 2018 – one geographical and two related to women in office. Of the latter two, one was a church requesting to join a classis that seats women and another was a church requesting to join a classis that does *not* seat women.[10] So, the CRCNA's position on women in office – which allows for two different convictions and interpretations of Scripture – has had an impact on the understanding of the classis and how it functions, and has led to transfers that stretch the geographic understanding of a classis. It also exemplifies a trend toward synodical decisions made for the whole denomination that allow for variations in local or regional implementation of the decision.

The tension between synodical authority and local control or local implementation that is evident in this matter has always been present in the CRCNA's Church Order. Article 27 displays that tension: one part of it comes from the DCO, saying 'the classis has the same authority over the council as the synod has over the classis', while its other subpoint says, 'each assembly exercises, in keeping with its own character and domain, the ecclesiastical authority entrusted to the church by Christ; the

---

7 *Acts of Synod 1995*, 733.
8 *Acts of Synod 2007*, 608.
9 As of 2018, three classes (Heartland, Illiana, Minnkota) do not allow women delegates at all, and one (Yellowstone) does not allow women minister delegates, but does allow women elders and deacons.
10 *Agenda for Synod 2018*, 307–312.

authority of councils being original, that of major assemblies being delegated'.[11]

Most in the CRCNA today seem to lean toward the latter view, that the classis has authority only as delegated to it by the churches, and very little hierarchical authority. This also fits with the shift toward the newer *koinōnia* understanding of the classis and away from the episcopal understanding. Many classes today do much more than the 'business' of classis. They spend time in worship and prayer, hold educational sessions and discussions of ministry issues, engage in joint ministries in their regions, and sometimes hire employees for that work. The CRCNA Church Order's Article 41 used to contain a list of items that the churches had to check on their credentials to ensure they were performing their duties properly, a sign of *episkopē*; today it focuses on responding to requests for help or advice from the churches and allowing time for discussion of ministry issues,[12] a sign of *koinōnia*.

Further, the roles of classical functionaries are changing. Church visitors are being re-trained as coaches and encouragers, rather than as evaluators. Regional pastors and mentors focus on guiding pastors in ministry and giving them support. These new emphases may be more fitting in the 21st century North American context, but there still is a need for the episcopal function of the classis, since the 'business' of the churches needs to be done and the approvals for various decisions are required. There also is some resistance to the newer functions and to the classis renewal movement among those who would prefer to maintain the episcopal function.

The ecclesiological vision in the CRCNA
The ecclesiological vision of the CRCNA, as displayed in the classis, is shifting from a gathering of office-bearers to 'do the business' of the church to a gathering of the regional church in *koinōnia* – a body that worships, learns together, encourages fellowship and care, and sponsors regional ministries. So, in that sense, the classis is acting more and more like a church! If the mission of the church is to gather in worship, nurture faith, offer pastoral care, and reach out with the gospel, then the classis is becoming more missional. This is a new understanding of the 'task and activities' of the church, which is one of the four main sections of the

---
11 *Church Order and its Supplements 2018*, 47.
12 *Church Order and its Supplements 2018*, 84.

CRCNA's Church Order, and includes the four sub-categories of worship, faith nurture, pastoral care, and ministries of the church.[13]

The CRCNA has been moving toward a more meaningful experience of the classis as a healthy structure that promotes fellowship and ministry, one that has been built up by years of efforts toward classis renewal, beginning in the 1990's. This movement sought to 'support the development of vibrant classes to enhance local church growth and community ministry',[14] thereby addressing some unhealthy patterns in classes that were declining in size and in enthusiasm for ministry. Craig Van Gelder's chapter, "Looking Back, Seeing Forward," in the above-referenced book from the conference on the classis in 2008 had identified the need to change this ecclesiological understanding due to changing contexts in this century, certainly very different from the Synod of Dort in 1618-1619, and from the CRCNA's Synod of 1881 that adopted the DCO as its own.[15]

Van Gelder noted that the DCO ended with Article 86 saying that 'these articles, related to the lawful order of the church, have been so drafted and adopted by common consent, that they, if the profit of the church demand otherwise, may and ought to be altered, augmented, or diminished'.[16] This indication of openness to change is reflective of John Calvin's view in Book IV of his Institutes, in which he writes that because 'these things are not necessary for salvation, and for the upbuilding of the church ought to be variously accommodated to the customs of each nation and age, it will be fitting (as the advantage of the church will require) to change and abrogate traditional practices and to establish new ones'.[17] Van Gelder points out that this flexibility is actually less prominent in the CRCNA's Church Order today, and has been so since the major revision of 1965, when Article 86 became, "This Church Order, having been adopted by common consent, shall be faithfully observed, and any revision thereof shall be made only by synod."[18]

The truth of the matter is that changes to the Church Order have become much more frequent since the full revision approved by Synod 1965; indeed, almost every year some adjustment is adopted, largely due

---

13 *Church Order and its Supplements 2018*, 90–98.
14 *Agenda for Synod 2018*, 45.
15 Janssen/Van den Broeke, *A Collegial Bishop?*, 111–134.
16 Janssen/Van den Broeke, *A Collegial Bishop?*, 126.
17 Calvin, *Institutes of the Christian Religion* IV.X.30, 1208.
18 Janssen/Van den Broeke, *A Collegial Bishop?*, 126.

to the changing contexts of churches and ministry in North America. Gradually, the Church Order is becoming more fitting for a 21st century church that is desiring *koinōnia* in addition to the necessary accountability of the episcopal function. Perhaps this is not an 'either/or' question, but a 'both/and' answer!

The shift in emphasis and understanding is especially demonstrated by the revisions adopted by Synod 2015, recommended by the Task Force to Study the Offices of Elder and Deacon.[19] These changes went beyond the intended enhanced understanding of the office of deacon and added a ministry focus to several other parts of the Church Order. For instance, Article 1 gained a reference to Ephesians 4:12, in addition to I Corinthians 14:40, so that the purpose of the Church Order is noted as not only to regulate the church 'in a fitting and orderly way', (*episkopē*); but also 'to prepare God's people for works of service, so that the body of Christ may be built up', (*koinōnia*, as well as *episkopē*).[20]

Furthermore, Articles 73 to 77, formerly titled the 'Mission of the Church' were changed to focus on the "Ministries of the Church," including the ministries of all the offices, and Article 75 was changed to require classes to 'implement a ministry plan that advances evangelistic and diaconal witness to Christ and his kingdom in its specific region and, when necessary, assist those churches needing support to fulfill their mission'.[21] This was a result of years of classis renewal efforts, finally being codified in the Church Order, interestingly, originating from an effort to revitalize the office of deacon, now included in all of the assemblies of the church: local councils, regional classes, and the denominational synod.

Synod 2015 had also appointed another Classis Renewal Group to build on the work of Classis Renewal which had been developing since the 1990's, including conferences, teams, and coaching at the classical level, as well as staff on the classical and denominational levels to support these efforts.[22] The group appointed in 2015 was charged with 'an examination of the nature, scope, and purpose of classes, with the objective of boldly exploring and innovatively addressing revisions to structures and to the Church Order that will enable classes to flourish'.[23] The carrying out of

---

19 *Agenda for Synod 2015*, 380–410.
20 *Acts of Synod 2015*, 658–659.
21 *Church Order and its Supplements 2018*, 96.
22 *Agenda for Synod 2018*, 45.
23 *Acts of Synod 2016*, 680.

this new vision was exhibited in their report to Synod 2018, which identified the fourfold purpose of the classis as 'a place of discerning the Spirit in community', 'a network of support and accountability', 'living into a collective calling', and 'a connection to the wider church'.[24] Those purposes are evidence of the growing emphasis on *koinōnia*.

The report of the Classis Renewal Group culminated in a proposed change to Church Order Article 39 that alters the definition of the classis. In addition to the statement that 'a classis shall consist of a group of neighboring churches', it adds: 'a classis is a group of Christian Reformed churches that comes together to seek, discern, and submit to God's will; offer one another mutual support and accountability; find ways to live out a collective calling within their region; and allow for a healthy and sustained connection to the wider denomination'.[25] One church sent an overture to Synod 2018 objecting to this change, claiming that classes were not sufficiently consulted regarding the change, and asked synod not to adopt it, since it is a substantive change. This ran contrary to the judgment of the Council of Delegates (the interim committee of synod) that had recommended immediate adoption and implementation, since the change was not substantive.[26] Synod 2018 agreed with the overture and decided to recommend adoption to Synod 2019, arguing that the change is substantive.[27] In fact, the change, if adopted, would signify the shift from an understanding of the classis as *episkopē* to that of *koinōnia*.

Ironically, another overture came to Synod 2018 from a different classis asking for a name change – to change the name of the classis to 'regional assembly', on the ground that 'regional assembly' is easier to understand than the term 'classis', which is considered archaic and confusing by some.[28] However, it should be noted that the phrase 'regional assembly' harkens back to the episcopal function of the classis more than the *koinōnia* function, since it designates a meeting of a group of people representing the churches in the region. So, this proposal could be seen as going in a different direction than the classis renewal movement. Synod 2018 referred the proposal to the Council of Delegates and the Classis Renewal Advisory Team for analysis of the terminology and the financial

---

24 *Agenda for Synod 2018*, 46. Full report, 44–50.
25 Ibid., 50.
26 *Acts of Synod 2018*, 409–411.
27 Ibid., 518.
28 *Agenda for Synod 2018*, 314–315.

and legal ramifications of the change. Further grounds noted that 'more conversation needs to happen about what terminology would communicate clearly and effectively while remaining sensitive to our history', and 'the phrase *regional assembly* may not be the most appropriate title given current developments such as the proposed definition of a classis and the movement of congregations to classes that are not in their geographical region'.[29]

It is interesting that in 2018, the start of the 400th anniversary of the Synod of Dordt, the CRCNA is considering a different understanding of the classis, one that is more fitting for the North American 21st century context, even as it considers a new name for the classis. It may be time to acknowledge both the benefits and the limitations of the language of the DCO and move on to the next stage of the *koinōnia* understanding of the classis: a focus on ministry in the missional church, and a focus on office that, as Van Gelder suggested, begins with the office of the believer and builds on the relationships between leaders and congregants.

The relationship between the classis and the leadership of the CRCNA

In an age of declining support for denominations, the leaders of the CRCNA have been focusing on serving the classes and churches, both to strengthen those local churches and to encourage their giving to the denomination through ministry shares, the CRCNA's system for collecting assessments from churches to share in the support of denominational ministries. Those efforts are extended to classes through grants that are available for renewal projects, and resources and advice available through trained denominational personnel. Denominational leaders also offer orientation and training for classical functionaries (stated clerks especially, but also synodical deputies, church visitors, and regional pastors) because often there is so little institutional memory and understanding of our polity, and because classis leaders sometimes go their own way without consulting the guidance of the Church Order.

Along with these trends, classis renewal efforts have now been lodged in a denominational staff person available to resource classes, encourage them, and work toward the *koinōnia* vision of the regional church. This classis renewal consultant's responsibility is to support classes and 'to recommend next steps in creating a healthy denominational structure with a vibrant middle judicatory'.[30]

---

29 *Acts of Synod 2018*, 454.
30 *Agenda for Synod 2018*, 46.

However, finding capacity for this work can be problematic. Members of the churches in a classis are not always willing and able to give time to the work of the classis. Hiring staff to run those classical ministries may then be a technical solution to an adaptive challenge, which offers a quick fix, but avoids the necessary work that requires classis delegates themselves to change and engage in the regional ministries. Further, there is some concern that the proposals brought to Synod 2018 from the Classical Renewal Group were produced by denominational staff, and not by the classes themselves. In fact, one church's overture to Synod 2018 objected to the Group's recommendation that classes be held accountable to create and implement their ministry plans.[31] So, the episcopal function is being used to regulate the *koinōnia* function!

One wonders how this will all work out in a denomination that allows relative independence among its classes, and even tolerates resistance to synod's decisions. There are plenty of examples of classical independence, when classes go their own way and sometimes disregard synodical decisions and the Church Order and its provisions, knowing enforcement is not likely to happen.[32] For example, one classis adopted the Belhar Confession as a fourth confession, even though the CRCNA's synod had not, and is engaged in international church planting, though synod strongly cautioned against that activity. Some classes admonish their ministers for dedicating infants rather than baptizing them; other classes allow the practice to go unchallenged, even though synod has been clear that ministers should not replace infant baptism with infant dedication. One classis sent an overture to synod to allow a classis *contracta*, which is a contracted classis meeting, requiring 'a quorum of half of the churches of a classis plus one',[33] for all candidate examinations, because of the large number of examinations that occurred in their classis, leading to many extra classis meetings. Synod said no to the overture,[34] but the classis went ahead and has made it their practice anyway, requiring only some of its churches to send delegates to these special meetings, rather than all of the churches in the classis. Some classes allow churches to not send deacon delegates even though the Church Order requires it. Many classes tend to be sympathetic to ministry leaders'

---

31 *Acts of Synod 2018*, 409–411.
32 The following examples were gleaned over time through the author's reading of various classical agendas and minutes.
33 *Church Order 2018*, 83.
34 *Acts of Synod 2015*, 674.

concerns and preferences, and reluctant to stress the episcopal function of the classis.

On the other hand, one classis has tried to heighten the episcopal function by asking synod to enforce discipline of those classes and churches that it perceives as out of bounds in some of their decisions or lack of action on disciplinary matters. This request was denied because discipline is implemented locally and goes to the broader assemblies only upon appeal.[35] Then, this classis sent an overture to synod proposing a change to the Church Order related to appeals so that one classis could appeal another's decisions, thereby functioning as a 'lateral' supervisory bishop. Synod 2018 did not accede to this overture, realizing it was not in the best interest of either *koinōnia* or good order, and retained the practice of only allowing appeals that go to the next assembly in line.[36] So the CRCNA may be balancing tensions as it works to create healthy classes, but the tensions are very real.

Conclusions
Overall, as mentioned above, the classes of the CRCNA are leaning toward the *koinōnia* understanding of the classis in their practices and may continue to do so under a new definition of the classis, if adopted by Synod 2019. This seems to be a good development for the health of the churches and the classes, remembering that the episcopal functions of the classis need to be accomplished as well. Synod 2019 adopted the revision to Article 39 and the new definition and understanding of the classis, but did not adopt the proposal to change the name of the classis to the regional assembly. It will be very interesting to see what happens in the years to come!

Bibliography
Acts of Synod 1995. Grand Rapids, MI, Christian Reformed Church in North America, 1995.

Acts of Synod 1996. Grand Rapids, MI, Christian Reformed Church in North America, 1996.

Acts of Synod 2007. Grand Rapids, MI, Christian Reformed Church in North America, 2007.

---

35 *Acts of Synod 2011*, 873.
36 *Acts of Synod 2018*, 516.

Acts of Synod 2015. Grand Rapids, MI, Christian Reformed Church in North America, 2015.

Acts of Synod 2016. Grand Rapids, MI, Christian Reformed Church in North America, 2016.

Acts of Synod 2018. Grand Rapids, MI, Christian Reformed Church in North America, 2018.

Calvin, John. *Institutes of the Christian Religion*. John T. McNeill, ed., Ford Lewis Battles, trans. Philadelphia: Westminster, 1960.

Church Order and its Supplements 2018. Grand Rapids, MI, Christian Reformed Church in North America, 2018.

Hall, David W. and Joseph H. Hall, eds. *Paradigms in Polity: Classic Readings in Reformed and Presbyterian Church Government*. Grand Rapids, MI: Wm. B. Eerdmans Publishing Co, 1994.

Janssen, Allan J., and Leon van den Broeke, eds. *A Collegial Bishop? Classis and Presbytery at Issue*. Grand Rapids, MI: Wm. B. Eerdmans Publishing Co., 2010.

Classis in the Evangelical Church of Czech Brethren

Adam Csukás

Introduction

The Evangelical Church of Czech Brethren (ECCB)[1] is a mainline Protestant denomination operating in the Czech Republic[2] and characterizing itself as a church with a presbyterial or presbyterial-synodical church polity.[3] The ECCB currently has 14 classes, including one that is non-territorial, and 251 local congregations. However, before reporting on the status of the classis in the ECCB, we have to pay attention to the specific historical development of the church polity of the ECCB, which differs significantly from traditional Presbyterianism.

It was a long and complicated journey from the beginnings of the Czech Reformation in the fifteenth century, through the persecution, toleration and formal equality of Czech Protestants in the Habsburg Empire and to the establishment of the ECCB in December 1918 following the collapse of Austria-Hungary under the rule of the Habsburgs, the declaration of independence of the Czechoslovak Republic and the end of the First World War.[4]

The church polity of today's ECCB consists of elements whose origin can be traced back to each of the aforementioned periods in the history of Czech Protestantism. As a result, discussion is ongoing as to whether the ECCB meets the necessary prerequisites of Presbyterian church government as it is known in the Netherlands, Scotland or the U.S.A.

---

1 This paper was prepared on the basis of full financial support from the Grant Agency of Charles University under GA UK project n°. 270218 "The Legal Order of the Evangelical Church of Czech Brethren – History and Present."
2 For more details on church and state relations in the Czech Republic, see Tretera/Horák, *Religion and Law in the Czech Republic*.
3 The preamble of the church constitution of the ECCB states that the church 'is governed by synodical-presbyterial principles'. In line with the other authors in this book I will make use of the term 'presbyterial-synodical'.
4 For a general overview of Czech legal history, see Kuklík, *Czech Law in Historical Contexts*.

The question is whether the ECCB has a Presbyterian church polity,[5] which traditionally attributes importance to the classis as the key judicatory of the denomination. In order to answer this question, we will pay attention to the particularities of the church polity of the ECCB, which are rooted in its historical development. For this reason, along with appropriate episodes in this development, we will consider the impact of historical and local circumstances on the church polity of the ECCB and its predecessors. Based on this knowledge, we will proceed to give an overview of the church polity of the ECCB. Finally, we will focus on the role of the classis within this denomination.

Heritage of the Czech Reformation
First, it is necessary to draw attention to the characteristic development of the Czech Reformation, which is associated with Jan Hus and the Hussite movement inspired by him, as well as with two denominations rooted in the fifteenth-century's Czech Reformation: the predominant Utraquist Church and the minority Unity of the Brethren.[6] With regard to the church polity of the ECCB, we must pay special attention to the latter church.

The Unity of the Brethren was established in the Czech countryside in 1457 and, from the very outset, placed great emphasis on church discipline. Its church polity was episcopal; however, apart from the bishops, there were both male and female elders. A few manuals for the elders have been preserved, providing strong evidence of the life within the discipline.[7] Since the 1580s, the Unity of the Brethren has leaned towards the theology of Calvinism,[8] but she has retained an episcopal church government.

Persecution of Czech Protestants
The Unity of the Brethren, as an organized religious community in the Czech lands, disappeared in the first third of the seventeenth century, following the Battle of the White Mountain in 1620, which marked the defeat of the Czech Estate Uprising against the Habsburgs, led by the Czech Protestant nobility, which in turn was followed by the re-Catholi-

---

5 For similar considerations in the context of the Hungarian Reformed Church see Szabó, "Does the Hungarian Reformed Church Have a Presbyterian System?" 173–185.
6 For more details, see Kejř, *The Hussite Revolution*.
7 See Říčan, *Die Böhmischen Brüder*, 205–224.
8 Ibid., 178–189.

cization of the Czech lands.[9] The Utraquists reunited with the Roman Catholic Church. The Unity of the Brethren disappeared into exile in the second half of the seventeenth century. Its last bishop, John Amos Comenius, died in Amsterdam in 1670.[10] For the next 160 years, the Protestants in the Czech lands were hard hit, especially the small scattered remnants of the Unity of the Brethren. Believers secretly met for worship in forests, caves or barns and were occasionally served by courageous foreign ministers, who brought them the Word and the sacraments.[11]

Toleration of Czech Protestants and Help from Abroad
Toleration of Protestants in the Czech lands was established under the domination of 'Enlightenment absolutism' in the 1780s, or, more precisely in 1781, when Emperor Joseph II published the Patent of Toleration for his crown lands, including Czech lands. 'The result of the declaration of the Patent of Toleration was marvellous', wrote church historian František Bednář; 'it was as if the graves had been opened and those who had long been considered dead, were emerging'.[12]

From 1781 to 1784, seventy-three Czech-speaking congregations were established in the Czech lands, of which fifty-four were of the Helvetic Confession (Reformed) and nineteen of the Augsburg Confession (Lutheran). The Protestants would have preferred to join the Czech and Brethren confessions from the age of the Czech Reformation, but the emperor ordered them to choose between the Helvetic and the Augsburg Confessions, of which they were unfamiliar. The number of Czech-speaking Protestants was around forty thousand during this period, which was, of course, remarkable because of the long period of persecution and their 'second-class' citizenship during the age of toleration.[13]

Czech Protestants had to wait until the second half of the nineteenth century for their first written church constitution, which was also octroyed. However, by the end of the eightteenth century, a new church

---

9   See Parma, "The Papacy and State Recatholicisation of the Czech Lands (1620–1740)," 185–208.
10 The Unity of the Brethren was restored in the 1720s in Herrnhut and is now also known as the Moravian Church. Although she is linked to the 'old' Unity of the Brethren, it has become another church. If we mention Unity of the Brethren in this paper, we mean the 'old' Unity of the Brethren established in 1457.
11 See Otter, *The Witness of Czech Protestantism*, 41.
12 Translated from Bednář, *Památník Českobratrské církve evangelické*, 17.
13 Ibid., 18–19.

polity began to be formed through the regulations of the emperor and his officers, although they greatly mistrusted the Protestants.[14]

However, we have to pay attention to the development of Protestant church law in the entire Habsburg Empire, including Hungary, where Protestants retained some of the rights they gained during the Estate Uprisings against the Habsburgs in the seventeenth century. As a consequence, their position in the 1780s was significantly better than that of Protestants in the Czech lands. After the Patent of Toleration was published in the Czech lands, several dozen Hungarian-speaking Reformed ministers and Slovak-speaking Lutheran ministers went to preach the Gospel in the Czech lands in the face of absolute uncertainty. They assumed the responsibility of newly established Czech congregations, experiencing difficult conditions.[15]

At the same time, when Czech Protestants were just establishing their congregations, Hungarian Protestants were facing the problem of their new church polity, which they had to create after decades of oppression. In the 1770s, Heinrich Gottfried Scheidemantel, a professor of feudal law at the University of Jena, was ordered by the Polish Reformed nobility to compile a church constitution. The Hungarian Reformed Church decided to take this constitution as their point of departure at the Synod of Buda in 1791, as did the Hungarian Lutheran Church at the Synod of Pest, which was simultaneously summoned. 'And it is unfortunate and strange that not the prosperous Presbyterian Protestant churches in Switzerland, the Netherlands or Scotland were taken as a model to follow', wrote church historian (and later bishop) Kálmán Révész, 'but they started off with the law code of the unfortunate neighbouring Polish dissident church that was torn by widespread trouble and discord, and vehemently sought to accommodate its institutions in the Hungarian Protestant churches living under other circumstances and with other requirements'.[16] The Hungarian Protestants' choice of the Polish code can be explained by their unfamiliarity with Presbyterian church polity, lack of time and the proximity of Hungary to Poland.

This time, the Hungarian Protestant nobility, who claimed credit in the struggles for the freedom of Protestants in the past, tried to eliminate

---

14 For more details, see Loesche, "Von der Duldung zur Gleichberechtigung;" Loesche, "Inneres Leben der Österreichischen Toleranzkirche."
15 See Révész, "Hungarian Protestantism in the Past," 49–50.
16 Translated from Révész, *A lengyel dissidens kánonok története s befolyása a budai zsinat törvényhozására*, 3.

ministers from church government in the Reformed and Lutheran Churches. As a result of the struggle between the *kyriarchy*, represented by the nobility, and the hierarchy, represented by the ministers, parity was established in the church polity of Hungarian Protestant Churches, whereby, in all higher judicatories, there had to be the same number of ministers and (ruling) elders.[17] Each level of church administration always required two representatives, namely, the minister and the curator,[18] which in Hungarian (*felügyelő* or *gondnok*) and Slovak (*dozorca*) literally means 'overseer' or 'guardian', in other words, *episkopos*.

Formal Equality of Czech Protestants Under State Control
The toleration of Protestants in the Czech lands changed to formal equality of Catholics and Protestants in 1861, when Emperor Francis Joseph issued his Protestant Patent. Following its publication, a 'provisional' octroyed church constitution of the Protestant Church in the Cisleithanian part of the Habsburg Empire (i.e., excluding Hungarian Kingdom) was published in the same year. The church constitution of 1861 and its revised versions from 1866, 1892 and 1913 (the revisions were adopted by the Synod) are in fact mixtures of two different approaches to a Protestant church polity – German and Hungarian.

Joseph Andreas Zimmermann, a German church law scholar of Protestant origin, born in Hungarian Transylvania, was the main author of the church constitution of 1861. He was well aware of the *kyriarchical* elements of the Hungarian Reformed church polity. Apart from this, he took a study trip in order to gain knowledge of the church polity in German lands.[19] He chose the Rhine-Westphalian Church Order of 1835[20] in the version that was in force in Baden in 1861[21] as a point of departure for the new constitution of the Protestant Church in Cisleithania.[22] This version, unlike the original from 1835, included the state consistory as a supreme governing body of the church. German consistorialism, with strong interference from the state in church matters, amalgamated with

---

17 For more details, see Zsedényi, "Hierarchie und Kyriarchie in der Verfassungsentwickelung der ungarländischen evangelischen Kirche A. B.", 626–642.
18 See Kováts, "Hungarian Protestantism Today", 69–70.
19 For more details, see Schwarz, "Providus et circumspectus," 181–207.
20 For more details, see Göbell, *Die Rheinisch-Westfälische Kirchenordnung vom 5. März 1835*.
21 See "Revise církevního zřízení", *Jednota* II, n°. 8 (1887), 117.
22 For more details, see Friedrich, *Einführung in das Kirchenrecht unter besonderer Berücksichtigung des Rechts der Evangelischen Landeskirche in Baden*, 175–181.

Hungarian parity of ministers and 'lay' church members in the higher judicatories, became a legal framework for Czech Protestants for the next 50 years.

Each branch of the church, i.e., Reformed and Lutheran, had its own local congregations gathered in classes and classes gathered in districts. Congregations, classes and districts had administrative and representative bodies: boards of elders and congregational assemblies, classical committees and classical assemblies, and district committees and district assemblies. Each branch finally had a General Synod with a committee comprising a few competences. In certain common matters, the General Synods could act together, but joint meetings were rare. The supreme administrative body of the Protestant Church in Cisleithania as a whole was the Imperial Royal Supreme Protestant Church Council (*Kaiserlich-königlicher evangelischer Oberkirchenrat*) in Vienna, a mixed authority that was both state and church in character. Members of the church council of both confessions were appointed by the emperor.[23]

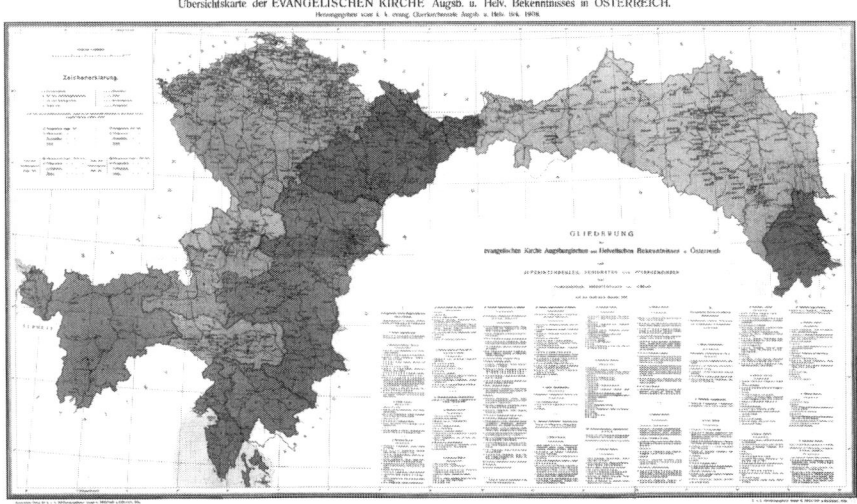

Map 1. Protestant Church in Cisleithania (1908)[24]

---

23 See Bednář, *Památník Českobratrské církve evangelické*, 50–58.
24 Kaiserlich-königlicher evangelischer Oberkirchenrat. Übersichtskarte der Evangelischen Kirche Augsb. u. Helv. Bekenntnisses in Österreich. 1:1,000,000.

Within the framework of the Protestant Church in Cisleithania, the Lutherans and the Reformed of several nations (German, Czech and Polish) co-existed. It is worth mentioning that most of the Czech Protestants were Reformed. Surely, the historical legacy of the Unity of the Brethren played a role in this. However, about a quarter of Czech Protestants were Lutherans. It is historically documented that some of the congregations mistakenly joined the Augsburg Confession; however, they chose to abide by it. While most of the Reformed, within the bounds of the Protestant Church in Cisleithania, were Czech-speaking, the vast majority of members of this church were German-speaking Lutherans.

The paradox of the Czech Reformed during this period was that, within the Protestant Church in Cisleithania, they constituted a great majority over the German Reformed; but, within the whole denomination, they constituted only a minority in relation to the German Lutheran majority. The church constitution was common, but the Czech Reformed Church did not have sufficient influence over its content. The Supreme Protestant Church Council was composed largely of German Lutherans, which meant that, when drafting the revised church constitution for the General Synod, it largely took on contemporary German patterns as its point of departure, which were remote from the traditional Presbyterianism of the Western Reformed Churches.

The resistance of the first generation of Czech Reformed ministers who studied abroad, especially in Switzerland, Scotland and the U.S.A., to German consistorialism and the un-Reformed church polity of the Protestant Church in Cisleithania, resulted in the Čáslav Constitutional Movement in the 1870s and 1880s, named after one of the Czech Reformed classes.

In the 1870s, a small group of highly educated Czech Reformed ministers drafted a proposal for a new church constitution, which was inspired primarily by the church polity of all three Scottish churches at that time, as well as the German Reformed Church in the U.S.A., which was, at that time, governed by a church constitution inspired by the DCO. About forty provisions of this church order were literally taken over by the Church Order of Čáslav, which was approved by the classes of the Czech-speaking Bohemian Reformed District and the district assembly. However, at the General Synod of the Reformed Church, which was held in Vienna in 1889, it was rejected by a majority of one vote because delegates from the sister Czech-speaking Moravian Reformed District voted against the proposal due to their down-to-earth attitude to the Supreme Protestant Church Council and the Cisleithanian government.

As far as its content was concerned, it was a very precise church order. Despite the foreign pattern, it was based on the 1866 church constitution of the Protestant Church in Cisleithania, but transformed to suit Reformed theology.[25]

Hundred Years of the Evangelical Church of Czech Brethren

The ECCB was established in December 1918, following the collapse of Austria-Hungary, the declaration of independence of the Czechoslovak Republic and the end of the First World War. The General Assembly of Czech Protestants declared the unification of Czech-speaking Reformed and Lutherans into one denomination, which was declared an heir to Jan Hus and the Czech Reformation by the General Assembly itself.

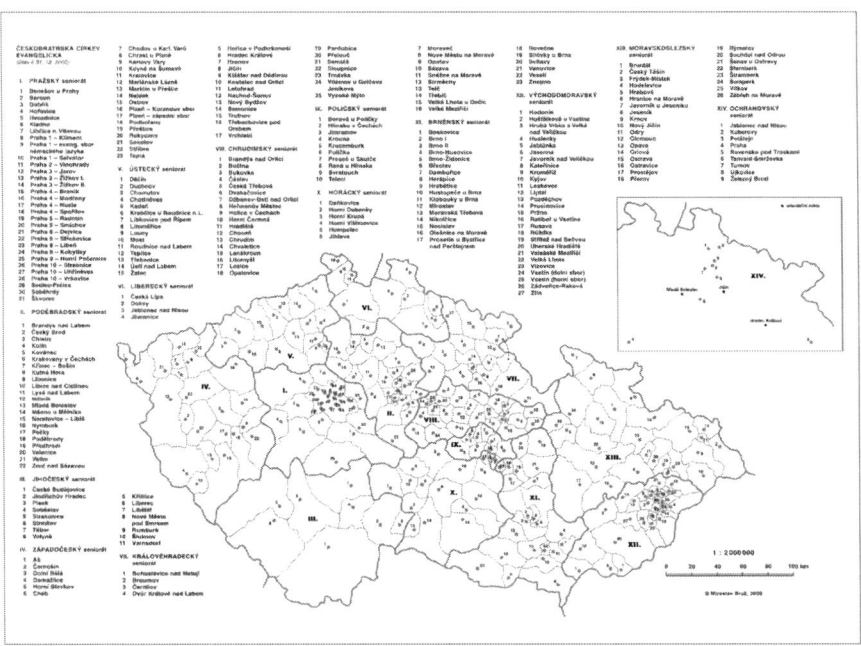

Map 2. *The Evangelical Church of Czech Brethren (2000)*[26]

---

25 See *Beilage zum Protokoll der VI. Böhmischen Superintendential-Versammlung H. C. vom Jahr 1881: Die Verfassung der reformirten Kirche Oesterreichs*, in the Central Archives of the ECCB, Prague, Czech Republic: Czech District H. C. (Box 73).
26 Brož, "Českobratrská církev evangelická (Stav k 31. 12. 2000)". 1:2,000,000.

Czechoslovakia formed an island of democracy and the rule of law in Central, Eastern and South-eastern Europe. It was the democratic system of the interwar Czechoslovak Republic that had a great impact on the first generation of leaders of the ECCB, while Presbyterianism became identified with secular democracy, evidence of which can be found in the first church constitution of the ECCB of 1922. The Supreme Protestant Church Council, appointed by the emperor, was replaced by the Synodical Committee, which was firstly elected by the General Assembly in December 1918, and subsequently by the Synod of the ECCB. Following the revision of the church constitution in 1929, the Synodical Committee was renamed the Synodical Council. Elders active in various societies and cooperatives have sometimes succumbed to the impression that even in the church everything can be decided by the voice of the majority. In some congregations, they went so far as to seek a vote on what the minister should preach and what to omit.

Democracy in the church, enacted in elections of all kinds and majority decision-making, played an important role, even after democracy in the state ceased to exist during the Second World War and the German occupation, as well as after 1948, when a forty-one-year Communist dictatorship was established in Czechoslovakia. Classical assemblies and the Synod were attended by the public in order to observe what a democracy looked like in a Western democratic parliament, because the Parliament of Czechoslovakia was only a puppet of the Communist Party.

In common with many Protestant denominations abroad, the ECCB also decided to revise her church constitution after the Second World War. Following seven years of preparations, a new church constitution was drafted and approved by the Synod in 1953. It entered into force in 1954 and, after many revisions, the most important of which took place in 1983 and the first half of the 1990s, is still in force today. The church constitution itself has been amended by several church orders dealing with special portions of church law, including church membership, vocation of ministers and procedure in judicatories.

The Church Constitution of the Evangelical Church of Czech Brethren
In summary, the organizational structure of the ECCB is threefold: local congregations, classes and the denomination itself. Each of these levels has an assembly, an administrative body and two representatives. The local congregation has its own assembly as well, while the governing body is the board of elders. The minister and curator are the representatives of the congregation. The classes have their own classical assemblies and

four- or six-member classical committees. Their representatives are the *seniores* and the classical curators. The assembly of the whole denomination is the Synod, while the governing body is the six-member Synodical Council. The representatives of the church are the Synodical *Senior* and the Synodical Curator.

Members of the classical assemblies and the Synod are elected for four years and the members of all administrative bodies are elected for six years. Their electoral periods are therefore not the same. Assemblies are usually held once a year and the administrative bodies meet once or twice a month. The representatives of the classes are always members of the classical committees and the Synod. All members of the Synodical Council are also automatically members of the Synod. The legal role of the representatives is primarily to represent the local congregations, the classes and the denomination outside the church, and all documents must be signed by both, otherwise they are null and void. However, their task within the church is of an administrative and ceremonial nature, rather than to govern.

This system of church government is well established. Interestingly, since the reform of the church constitution in the first half of the 1990s, the classical assemblies and the Synod need not be presided over by any of the representatives of the classes and the denomination, so as to prevent an accumulation of power.

When translating the title of the Synodical *Senior* into English, the term 'Moderator of the Synodical Council' is sometimes used. As noted, the Synodical *Senior* is not the Moderator of the Synod, despite the fact that he almost has the same position within the church as does, for example, the Moderator of the General Assembly in the Church of Scotland.

At present, too many tasks have been imposed on the Synodical Council, with a strengthening of the powers of the classical committees therefore envisaged. The administrative and technical background of the denomination is provided by the Central Church Office, which is managed by a stated clerk who is appointed by the Synodical Council. At present, about forty people are employed in the Central Church Office. Classes and congregations usually employ up to two employees.

Classis in the Evangelical Church of Czech Brethren
As stated above, we can find traces of each period of the history of Czech Protestantism in the church polity of the ECCB, including classes. So, how did the Unity of the Brethren influence the status of the classis in the current ECCB? The very name of the classis in Czech, namely the *seniorát*, is supposed to be of Brethren origin.

The desire for historical continuity with the Czech Reformation (and discontinuity with the development from 1781 to 1918) was manifested especially after the First World War. When Čeněk Dušek, a superintendent of the Czech Reformed District, died in November 1918, the contemporary church press wrote about his funeral:

> Hardly, I think, was there ever a funeral with greater participation, whether from church or non-church circles, as that at which the late superintendent was honoured. In addition to the home congregation, the burial ceremony was attended by members of Czech and Moravian congregations without distinction of confession. There were about 40 ministers in the Geneva gown. […] Thus, the last superintendent of the Czech Reformed Church was taken to his final rest place with an honour that reflected his importance. *Last, because the objective of the church in these new free times is to restore the old Brethren orders and dignities.*[27]

Thus, renaming the office of superintendent and revising the respective competences was considered as proof of a new age. The bishops in the Unity of the Brethren were known as *seniores*. This term had been used in Cisleithania since the 1780s for naming representatives of the classes from the ranks of the ministers. The first church constitution of the ECCB in 1922 took the name after the Brethren pattern for the office of the Chairman of the Synodical Committee, because the term 'bishop' was considered inappropriate, especially due to the contemporary anti-Catholic mood among Czech Protestants. Classical representatives were renamed *conseniores*, again after the pattern of the Unity of the Brethren. *Senior* was renamed as Synodical *Senior* in 1929, while *conseniores* were renamed as *seniores*. The legacy of the Unity of the Brethren to the present church polity of the ECCB is therefore mainly terminological, since the content of the service of the *seniores* in the Unity of the Brethren, compared to today's ECCB, is quite different, as mentioned above.

The classes themselves were established in Cisleithania after the promulgation of the Patent of Toleration in 1781, following the decision of the emperor. *Seniores* were in fact considered as helpers of the superintendents, so their service during this era can be likened to that of vicars

---

27 Translated from "Pohřeb vdp. dra. Č. Duška v Kolíně", *Husův odkaz*, 6 January 1919, 10–11.

forane (*vicarii foranei*) in today's Roman Catholic Church.[28] The establishment of classical assemblies at this time was not even considered from the point of view of the government. The first three Czech Reformed classes, headed by *seniores*, were established in 1784, but classical assemblies were not allowed until 1861.

After 1861, classical assemblies gathered for the first time. However, their power was completely negligible compared to the Supreme Protestant Church Council. They could neither examine candidates for ministry nor discipline congregations; they could only debate. However, classical assemblies have systematically drawn attention to the shortcomings of the existing church constitution. The major initiative in this regard was the Church Order of Čáslav, which proposed a substantial approximation of the status of the classis in the Protestant Church in Cisleithania to the Western Presbyterian Churches. However, even the authors of the Church Order of Čáslav were critical of the outcome and aware that this was a compromise between the existing and the desired church polity: "If we were to present the proposal to the state churches in France or Scotland, which are our patterns, they would dismiss us with contempt for our *seniores*, superintendents and councils, and would call it prelate slavery."[29]

However, until the collapse of Austria-Hungary and the Protestant Church in Cisleithania, no substantial changes were made in the status of the classis. The revision of the church constitution from 1892 just led to a single change, that *seniores* and superintendents were no more elected by congregations, but by a classical assembly and a district assembly, respectively.

In 1917, when the Central Committee of Czech Protestants, comprising prominent church leaders of that time, leading finally to the unification of Czech Reformed and Lutherans in December 1918, initiated its activity, a constitutional committee was established, whose aim was to draft a church constitution for the new church. In the first stage of its activity from May 1917 to December 1918, reform of the church polity corresponding to Western Presbyterianism was pursued.

---

28 Vicar forane (*vicarius foraneus*) is a term of Catholic canon law, used also in the official English translation of the Code of Canon Law. Vicar forane stands between a bishop and a parish priest, in the terms of hierarchy, like rural deans in the Church of England; accessed 21 January 2020, https://www.vatican.va/archive/ENG1104/__P1V.HTM.

29 Translated from "Konvent čáslavský", *Jednota* III, n°. 10 (1888), 150.

However, after the declaration of independence of the Czechoslovak Republic on 28th October 1918 and after the General Assembly of Czech Protestants gathered in Prague in December 1918, democracy in the church asserted itself, which, for example, resulted in an unsuccessful attempt to abolish the automatic membership of ministers in the classical assemblies; however, this was a denial of the historical development of the classis abroad. In fact, the final version of the church constitution of the ECCB of 1922 continued the status of the classis as it was known in the previous constitutions of the Protestant Church in Cisleithania. The classis was still considered a transient link between the congregations and the Synod, as districts were withdrawn from the church constitution after 1922.[30] Even the church constitution of the ECCB of 1922 and 1954, in its later versions, including the current one, did not fully recognize the important role of the classis.

Today, however, the ECCB is increasingly aware of the importance of classes. The Strategic Commission, whose task is to process the proposal of the document 'Reformanda 2030: The Strategic Plan of the ECCB', proposes to the Synod a significant extension of the power of classical committees, thus bringing the ECCB closer to the church polity of the Presbyterian churches. It is, therefore, desirable that classical committees and classical assemblies soon become leading courts of the denomination.

Collegial Bishop?
Does the classis in the ECCB fulfil its episcopal role? In terms of classical assemblies, the answer is 'No'; nor has it ever done so. For example, candidates seeking ministry in the ECCB are historically examined by a special commission, which is appointed by the Synodical Council and not by a classical assembly. Another example is that church visitation is the task of classical committees and of the Synodical Council. Yet another example is the power of classical committees, in urgent cases, to dissolve boards of elders and appoint an administrative commission in the congregation.

In this context, however, we must point out the frequent misunderstanding that exists in the literature, in particular, with regard to the Hungarian Reformed Church, which is the best known among the 'episcopal' Reformed Churches. It is superficial and inaccurate to speak of an episcopal polity with regard to the Catholic Church, or even some

---

30 For more details see Csukás, "Ústavní počátky Českobratrské církve evangelické", in: *Revue církevního práva* XXIV, n°. 73–4 (2018), 67–95.

of the Lutheran Churches. Hungarian and Slovak Reformed bishops, or the Synodical *Senior* and *seniores* of the ECCB, are not bishops in the sense of the Catholic Church, or of some Lutheran Churches. Their powers are negligible.

If we want to ascribe an episcopal role to some of the bodies of these churches, it would be to the classical committees and Synodical councils that exist in the ECCB, as well as in the Hungarian and Slovak Reformed Churches, as a result of similar developments in church polities. These bodies are well tested and, in view of the low number of their membership, are more effective than assemblies. As collegial bodies, which consist of both ministers and (ruling) elders, the risk of the misuse of their power is minimized.

On the contrary, the classical assemblies and synods act as representative bodies that deal with the most serious questions of the denomination, while their role is generally accepted and respected. In addition, they perform a significant supervisory role over the administrative bodies.

Is the church polity of the ECCB Presbyterian and, if so, to what extent? We have shown that the church polity of the ECCB is *mixtum compositum*, consisting of elements of German and Hungarian Protestant church polity, with very few traces of the traditional Presbyterian church polity, which has been always considered as a pattern worth following, but in fact was never followed.

Being 'presbyterial-synodical' under Hungarian conditions simply refers to the parity of ministers and non-ministers in higher judicatories, and parity in the representation of congregations, classes, districts and the whole denomination, when the minister (a *senior*, a bishop or a general bishop) is accompanied by a curator, whose office is widely respected as an office of the guardian of the church.[31]

Being 'presbyterial-synodical' in German recalls the Rhine-Westphalian Church Order of 1835 and all its revisions, which still represents the 'skeleton' of many of the Protestant Churches in German-speaking countries. These constitutions are characterized by the dualism of representative and administrative bodies at all levels of church administration, which may resemble secular democracy in some respects.[32]

---

31 See Szabó, "Does the Hungarian Reformed Church Have a Presbyterian System?," 173–185.
32 See Coertzen, *Decently and in Order*, 234–237, 242–244.

The church polity of the ECCB is therefore undoubtedly 'presbyterial-synodical' in the sense of German and Hungarian Protestant church polity. Her being 'Presbyterian' in the sense of traditional Western Presbyterianism is questionable. However, current developments in the church polity of some churches, for example, the Protestant Church in the Netherlands, where the office of *classispredikant*, similar to that of *senior* or the Synodical *Senior* in the ECCB, was introduced in 2018, as well as a significant reform of classes, show us that the needs of Protestant Churches in Europe are converging, despite their different historical development.

Bibliography

"Konvent čáslavský". *Jednota* III, n°. 10 (1888), 147–151.

"Pohřeb vdp. dra. Č. Duška v Kolíně". *Husův odkaz*, 6 January, 1919.

"Revise církevního zřízení". *Jednota* II, n°. 8 (1887), 117–118.

Bednář, František. *Památník Českobratrské církve evangelické*. Prague: Kalich, 1924.

Brož, Miroslav. Českobratrská církev evangelická (Stav k 31. 12. 2000)." 1:2,000,000. In *Církev v proměnách času*: 1969–1999. Prague: Kalich, 2002.

Coertzen, Pieter. *Decently and in Order: A Theological Reflection on the Order for, and the Order in, the Church*. Leuven: Peeters, 2004.

Csukás, Adam. "Ústavní počátky Českobratrské církve evangelické". *Revue církevního práva* XXIV, n°. 73–4 (2018), 67–95.

Friedrich, Otto. *Einführung in das Kirchenrecht unter besonderer Berücksichtigung des Rechts der Evangelischen Landeskirche in Baden*. Göttingen: Vandenhoeck & Ruprecht, 1961.

Göbell, Walter. *Die Rheinisch-Westfälische Kirchenordnung vom 5. März 1835*. Duisburg: Otto Hecker, 1948.

Kaiserlich-königlicher evangelischer Oberkirchenrat. *Übersichtskarte der Evangelischen Kirche Augsb. u. Helv. Bekenntnisses in Österreich.* 1:1,000,000. Wien: Freytag & Berndt, 1908.

Kejř, Jiří. *The Hussite Revolution.* Prague: Orbis, 1988.

Kováts, István J. "Hungarian Protestantism Today". In *Hungarian Protestantism: Its Past, Present and Future.* Budapest: Bethlen Gábor Literary and Priting House, 1927, 65–190.

Kuklík, Jan. *Czech Law in Historical Contexts.* Prague: Karolinum, 2015.

Loesche, Georg. "Inneres Leben der Österreichischen Toleranzkirche: Archivalische Beiträge zur Kirchen- und Sittengeschichte des Protestantismus in Österreich 1781–1861." *Jahrbuch der Gesellschaft für die Geschichte des Protestantismus in Österreich* 1915.

Loesche, Georg. "Von der Duldung zur Gleichberechtigung: Archivalische Beiträge zur Geschichte des Protestantismus in Österreich 1781–1861". *Jahrbuch der Gesellschaft für die Geschichte des Protestantismus in Österreich* 1911.

Otter, Jiří. *The Witness of Czech Protestantism.* Prague: Kalich, 1970.

Parma, Tomáš. "The Papacy and State Recatholicisation of the Czech Lands (1620–1740)." In *The Papacy and the Czech Lands: A History of Mutual Relations.* Prague: Institute of History, 2016, 185–208.

Révész, Imre. "Hungarian Protestantism in the Past." In *Hungarian Protestantism: Its Past, Present and Future.* Budapest: Bethlen Gábor Literary and Priting House, 1927, 1–62.

Révész, Kálmán. *A lengyel dissidens kánonok története s befolyása a budai zsinat törvényhozására.* Pápa: Debreczeny Károly, 1887.

Říčan, Rudolf. *Die Böhmischen Brüder.* Berlin: Union Verlag, 1961.

Schwarz, Karl W. "Providus et circumspectus: Der siebenbürgisch-sächsische Kirchenrechtspraktiker Joseph Andreas Zimmermann." In *Siebenbürgen in der Habsburgermonarchie: Vom Leopoldinum bis zum Ausgleich (1690-1867)*. Cologne–Weimar–Vienna: Böhlau Verlag, 1999, 181–207.

Szabó, István. "Does the Hungarian Reformed Church Have a Presbyterian System?" In *The Ministry of the Elders in the Reformed Churches*. Berne: Evangelische Arbeitsstelle Oekumene Schweiz, 1992, 173–185.

Tretera, Jiří Rajmund, and Záboj Horák. *Religion and Law in the Czech Republic*. 2nd ed. Alphen aan den Rijn: Kluwer Law International, 2017.

Zsedényi, Béla. "Hierarchie und Kyriarchie in der Verfassungsentwickelung der ungarländischen evangelischen Kirche A. B." In *Gedenkbuch anlässlich der 400-jährigen Jahreswende der Confessio Augustana*. Leipzig: Kommissionsverlag von Bernh. Liebisch, 1930, 541–676.

How Polity Dies: Form without Substance in the Presbyterian Church (U.S.A.)

Joseph D. Small

Presbyters shall come together in councils in regular gradation. These councils are sessions, presbyteries, synods, and the General Assembly. All councils of the church are united by the nature of the church and share with one another responsibilities, rights, and powers as provided in the Constitution. The councils are distinct but have such mutual relations that the act of one of them is the act of the whole church performed by it through the appropriate council. The larger part of the church, or a representation thereof, shall govern the smaller.
Foundations of Presbyterian Polity

Here I will confess, if that's the appropriate word, I myself am a lapsed Presbyterian. It's the diction that did it, finally, the worn-thin, shabby, church-poor words, so overused they connote to me a poverty of spirit, not the richness of it.
E.L. Doctorow, The Waterworks

Introduction

It is an enduring myth of American Presbyterianism that its form of government provided a model for the American government's system of representative legislative bodies. In the way the story is told, the church's democratically elected sessions, presbyteries, synods, and general assembly shaped their governmental counterparts in democratically elected town councils, state legislatures, and the United States Congress. It is a pleasant fable, but a fable nonetheless. Recently, however, the myth has lost its appeal. The degrading of American political life since the mid-1990s has led Presbyterians to downplay our fanciful role in the formation of the nation's federal system.

Our demythologizing has a drawback, however. It has enabled us to avoid recognition of our fable's flip side: the ways in which the American political system's disfunction shapes and reinforces the current practice of Presbyterian polity. Although we no longer call presbyteries and the general assembly 'governing bodies' or 'courts', we continue to mimic

American political life, legislating, regulating, and litigating, complete with the trappings of special interest lobbying and recourse to the judiciary. In all of this, we remain blissfully unaware that while our ecclesiastical system retains its form, it is being drained of its substance.

Several years ago, the Presbyterian Church (U.S.A.) [Hereafter PCUSA] radically revised its constitutional 'Form of Government', reducing its bulk, eliminating constricting regulations, providing space for ecclesial and pastoral judgment, and providing a theological basis, 'Foundations of Presbyterian Polity'. The outcome of this admirable revision has been modest, however. Church sessions go their own way, as they always have. Most synods no longer play a meaningful role. Tellingly, many presbyteries and the general assembly continue to operate as legislative and regulatory bodies as if nothing had changed.

Neglect of polity revision is a consequence of the church's customary neglect of polity itself. In the PCUSA, ecclesiastical polity is routinely pushed to the sidelines of seminary education and pastoral attention. The *Book of Order*[1] is generally viewed as a quick reference guide when difficult questions or potential problems arise, and as a procedural instrument to accomplish legislative and regulatory aims. Too little attention is given to its more basic, theological function in the life of the church.

This ought to be surprising. God's Way in the world with Israel and with the church is with a people, a community. And so, with Israel and with the church, the seemingly mundane matter of how the community is organized has been a determining element in how God's people understand the faithful shape of covenantal life.

In the church's life throughout time and place, preserving and transmitting apostolic faith, proclaiming the gospel and celebrating the sacraments, shaping public and personal righteousness, and coordinating mission in and to the world have never happened automatically. Communion in the faith and communion among the faithful require patterned relationships, and so Christian community requires structured ecclesial life. Church order is not a peripheral concern, but a central ecclesiological matter.

---

1 The Church's Constitution consists of *The Book of Confessions* and the *Book of Order* [Form of Government, Directory for Worship, and Rules of Discipline]. However, it is the Form of Government that reigns supreme.

The Devolution of Presbyterian Polity

The devolution of Presbyterian polity in the United States has been a long process, born of old disputes over theological and moral issues that led to periodic splits – in the nineteenth century: Old Side/New Side, Old School/New School, North/South. The past eighty years have seen four departures from the parent church – the Orthodox Presbyterian Church in the 1930s, the Presbyterian Church in America in the 1970s, the Evangelical Presbyterian Church in the 1980s, and the Covenant Order of Evangelical Presbyterians in the 2000s. In all of this, Presbyterian polity was not only incapable of preserving unity, it contributed to disunity. George Marsden's study of the shaping of twentieth century evangelicalism notes that, "Presbyterian harmony seemed to occur only in brief interludes between controversies." Why was this the case? Marsden continues:

> Presbyterians had developed organizational machinery for dealing with differences through a series of ecclesiastical courts (…). These courts, together with the perennial presence of a conservative party ready to prosecute doctrinal sins of either omission or commission, reduced the chances that Presbyterians would let theological differences coexist, or sleeping dogmas lie.[2]

Mainstream Presbyterians may be tempted to place all blame on 'the conservative party', but the underlying problem has been 'organizational machinery for dealing with differences through a series of ecclesiastical courts'. Presbyterian polity assumes that theological and moral disputes are to be resolved through democratic procedure, preeminently by voting, which guarantees that there will be theological and moral winners and losers. C.P. Snow, British scientist and keen observer of culture, observed that, "The number 2 is a very dangerous number (…). Attempts to divide anything by two ought to be regarded with much suspicion."[3]

Snow's observation should ring true in Presbyterian ears. The divisive issues of the past decades – the place of gay and lesbian persons in the church, abortion, Israel-Palestine, church property rights, Christology and the doctrine of the Trinity, climate change, and more – have been made intractable by their reduction to two opposing positions. Even our best-intentioned discussions reinforce polar divisions by guaranteeing a voice to 'both sides of the issue' (…) as if any issue worth discussing has

---

2 Marsden, *Fundamentalism and American Culture*, 109.
3 Snow, *The Two Cultures and a Second Look*, 9.

only two sides. Our polity presses us toward legislative dualisms as every matter is reduced to a vote: yes or no, up or down. Having divided ourselves into two camps, we should not be surprised by the absence of common ground.

It is not my purpose to critique democratic proceduralism; I have done that elsewhere.[4] Instead, I want to examine the existential problem faced by American Presbyterian polity: that its own chosen and carefully crafted democratic procedures are being drained of their substance. The church's method of making decisions and resolving disputes is becoming a hollowed-out instrument, often failing to make decisions that the whole church embraces, and incapable of resolving ensuing disputes. The church's existential problem is less about democratic procedure itself than the underlying norms that make democratic procedure possible.

How Democracies Die
A recent book, *How Democracies Die*, examines the ways democratic governments throughout the world have collapsed. The book sets out the historical reality that democratic governments do not always die by hostile takeover. Revolutions and *coups d'état* have destroyed their share of democracies, but democracies often die by a gradual erosion of the institutions and cultural norms that give substance to the framework of democratic procedure. Authors Steven Levitsky and Daniel Ziblatt analyze numerous instances where democracies have died slowly, often in barely discernible steps. Sometimes, they write, subversions of democracy 'are "legal," in the sense that they are approved by the legislature or accepted by the courts. They may even be portrayed as efforts to *improve* democracy – making the judiciary more efficient, combatting corruption, or cleaning up the electoral process'.[5] Nevertheless, whether formally or unofficially, the result is the subversion of democratic standards and practices (witness Venezuela, Hungary, and Russia, among others).

Levitsky and Ziblatt, with Donald Trump clearly in mind, are concerned with cases where political leaders willfully delegitimize and undermine democratic values and procedures. I, however, do not have church villains in mind; I do not believe that Presbyterian leaders intentionally subvert democracy in the church (although some

---
4 See Small, "The Democratic Captivity of the Church,"; and "Presbyterianism's Democratic Captivity," *First Things*, n°. 221, March, 2012.
5 Levitsky/Ziblatt. *How Democracies Die*, 5.

unintentional actions by ecclesiastical leaders have undermined democratic performance in the church). What interests me in Levitsky and Ziblatt's book is their discussion of the unwritten norms that are essential to democracy's functioning. These norms, say the authors, are 'shared codes of conduct that become common knowledge within a particular community or society – accepted, respected, and enforced by its members. Because they are unwritten, they are often hard to see, especially when they're functioning well'.[6] The authors characterize such norms as 'the soft guardrails of democracy, preventing day-to-day political competition from devolving into a no-holds-barred conflict'.[7]

Two norms are identified as fundamental to democracy's functioning: *mutual toleration* and *institutional forbearance*. Neither is a goal of democracy; toleration and forbearance are the cultural presuppositions that make democratic functioning possible by serving as 'guardrails' that prevent democracy from careening off the road. When these fundamental norms are operative, they are as taken for granted as the air we breathe; when they are absent, their indispensability becomes apparent.

Within a nation, an organization, a community, or a church, *mutual toleration* signals the understanding that as long as rivals play by the rules, each accepts that the others have an equal right to exist, compete for influence, and govern. While rivals may strongly disagree with, even dislike, each other, each accepts the other as legitimate. Mutual toleration does not mean ignoring differences as if they did not matter, but rather engaging differences in the bond of mutual respect. Mutual toleration means that, 'even if we believe our opponents' ideas to be foolish or wrong-headed, we do not view them as an existential threat. Nor do we treat them as treasonous, subversive, or otherwise beyond the pale'.[8] Tolerance is often thought to be a weak concept, falling short of deep mutual relationships. Yet deep mutual relationships are impossible apart from the minimal foundation of mutual toleration. Tolerance is not a goal of ecclesial life, but rather its indispensable presupposition.

The second norm critical to democracy's survival is *institutional forbearance*, a form of corporate self-control that restrains an institution, its sub-sets, and its leaders from exercising fully certain legitimate rights. Institutional forbearance does not mean capitulation to a minority position. Rather, as Levitsky and Ziblatt say, '[it] can be thought of as

---

6 Ibid., 102.
7 Ibid., 101.
8 Ibid., 102.

avoiding actions that, while respecting the letter of the law, obviously violate its spirit. Where norms of forbearance are strong, politicians do not use their institutional prerogatives to the hilt, even if it is technically legal to do so, for such action could imperil the existing system'.[9] Those in control refrain from fully exercising power over a rival minority, especially in situations when to do so would endanger the unity of the whole.

It is precisely these two foundational norms that have been weakened in the PCUSA. The soft guardrails of Presbyterian polity have fallen into disrepair, no longer strong enough to prevent the possibility of institutional wreckage. It is instructive to note that within the Presbyterian system there is an inverse relationship between these norms and democratic proceduralism. Where voting is least important (session) tolerance of difference and forbearance are regularly exercised. Where voting is the name of the game (general assembly) intolerance of opponents and legal imposition are most in evidence. The PCUSA's 171 presbyteries vary in all of this, but too many of them are also characterized by mutual intolerance and institutional compulsion.

The Waning of Mutual Tolerance
The history of Presbyterian controversies in the twentieth and early twenty-first centuries is complex and does not lend itself to easy generalizations. Even so, it can be said that the Presbyterian version of the 1910-1936 'Fundamentalist-Modernist controversy' signaled the onset of the current version of Presbyterian mutual intolerance and institutional coercion. Two vignettes from the controversy, both involving conservative combatant J. Gresham Machen, are instructive. The first involves the harsh, Manichaean rhetoric with which Machen battled his adversaries in the church. The second concerns the harsh, retributive response of the institutional church.

Machen was a professor at Princeton Seminary whose critique of both seminary and denomination was acerbic and inflammatory. His 1924 book, *Christianity and Liberalism* set the tone. It claimed that religious liberalism was 'un-Christian'. In fact, liberalism was so un-Christian that it could only be seen as, 'a religion which is so entirely different from Christianity as to belong in a distinct category'.[10] Un-Christian liberalism, wrote Machen, was 'The chief modern rival of Christianity', and 'An examination of the teachings of liberalism in comparison with those of

---

9 Ibid., 106.
10 Machen, *Christianity and Liberalism*, 6f.

Christianity will show at every point the two movements are in direct opposition'.[11]

Machen did not believe that the liberalism he contended against was a mere abstraction. In his view, liberal religion was a real and present existential threat within the Presbyterian Church. He contended that,

> The Church of to-day (sic) has been unfaithful to its Lord by admitting great companies of non-Christian persons, not only into her membership, but into her teaching agencies (…). Such persons have been admitted (…) to the ministry of the Church, and to an increasing extent have been allowed to dominate its councils and determine its teaching. The greatest menace to the Christian Church to-day comes not from the enemies outside, but from the enemies within.[12]

Machen perceived the danger to the church as life-threatening, and so, 'In the intellectual battle of the present day there can be no 'peace without victory'; one side or the other must win'.[13]

Machen was not alone in employing harsh judgmental rhetoric to critique adversaries within the church; liberals were swift to castigate Machen with their own invectives (although, stylistically, they failed to give as good as they got). But it was Machen's abrasive, accusatory rhetoric that set the tone for the conduct of conflicts that have characterized Presbyterian Church life since the 1960s.

The Presbyterian Church has experienced decades of contention over confessional revision, church and state, women in ministry, race, Scripture, property, abortion, Christology, human sexuality, ordination, Trinity, marriage, Scripture, and more. These disputes produced opposing special interest groups within the church that organized to influence church opinion and contend for votes in presbyteries and the general assembly. These groups, like lobbying groups in the national government, contributed to the reduction of complex matters to opposing alternatives. All of this hardened the terms and the tone of debate. On issue after issue, both official and informal, 'one side or the other must win' was the rallying cry of both 'sides'.

Mutual toleration – groups granting legitimacy and authenticity to groups with which they disagree – was undermined by back and forth

---

11 Ibid., 53.
12 Ibid., 161.
13 Ibid., 6.

denunciations: 'apostasy (…) homophobia (…) denial of biblical authority (…) racism (…) universalism (…) misogyny (…) dishonesty (…) heresy (…) schismatics (…) bibliolatry (…)' and on and on. Not all, not even most Presbyterians engaged in such contemptuous rhetoric, but organized public bipolarization and harsh characterizations hardened differences throughout the church, made the 'sides' mutually suspicious and dismissive, and guaranteed that the cost of victory would be high.

Nearly half a century of Presbyterian mutual intolerance has led to major divisions of the church in which those who departed accused the PCUSA of views and actions they could not tolerate, while many who remained within the PCUSA were pleased to see the departure of those whose views and actions they considered intolerable. In all of this, mutual tolerance was discarded as contenders failed to recognize validity and sincerity in one another, treated one another as violators of Christian faith and life, and labelled one another 'unacceptable'.

The Waning of Institutional Forbearance
The second guardrail of democracy is *institutional forbearance*, the refusal of those in organizational control to use all the means at their disposal to compel the accession of their rivals. Once again, the case of J. Gresham Machen was a harbinger of things to come.

Machen's attacks on liberalism in the church were a constant irritation to church leaders. The institutional response was to use its power to rid the church of 'this meddlesome priest'. Machen's meddling went beyond inflammatory books and speeches. Following a reorganization of Princeton Seminary to which he was opposed, Machen founded a new school, Westminster Seminary in Philadelphia. His critique of the Presbyterian Board of Foreign Missions led him to establish an independent mission board. Both the seminary and the mission board were minor undertakings, but both were considered unacceptable rivals by official Presbyterian institutions.

The Stated Clerk of the PCUSA counseled presbyteries not to license or ordain Westminster Seminary graduates, and further ruled that the new mission board subverted Presbyterian law by undertaking administrative functions apart from official oversight. A General Assembly study of Machen's mission board was authorized; it swiftly concluded that the independent mission board was contrary to the church's constitution. The study went so far as to assert that anyone who would not support the church's officially authorized missions board was in the same position with regard to church law as a church member who refused to take part in the celebration of the Lord's Supper or any of the other prescribed ordinances of the denomination![14] On this basis Machen was tried by his presbytery, convicted, and suspended from the ministry. He soon left to form his own denomination.

D.G. Hart, a historian sympathetic to Machen, observes that, 'one of the curious features of the Presbyterian controversy is why the denomination devoted so much energy to silencing what was at best a small and peripheral movement'.[15] Westminster Seminary graduated no more than eight students a year throughout the 1930s, many of whom were not Presbyterians. Machen's independent mission board appointed only eleven missionaries. When Machen formed the Orthodox Presbyterian Church, he was followed out of the PCUSA by no congregations and a mere thirty-four ministers and seventeen elders.[16] Machen's challenges to the institution attracted a small, marginal following, yet they were met by the maximum exercise of institutional power. This presaged the character of future denominational response.

In disputes over women in ministry, boycotts, race, ordination standards, church property, theological diversity, and more, whichever faction held the reins of power attempted to use the church's constitutional and juridical apparatus to force acquiescence: charges filed, constitutional amendment requirements bypassed, property rights used to punish, social witness policies multiplied, commissions undermined, budgets weaponized, and on and on. This has led to open disobedience by whichever faction is in the minority. This, in turn, has led to lawsuits in *civil courts*!

The Death of Polity
The upshot of all this is not the explicit overthrow of Presbyterian polity, but rather the attenuation of polity's intended purpose, resulting in diminished confidence in its capacity to address significant theological and moral matters. Polity and the instruments of polity – local, regional, and national councils – are being marginalized throughout the church. Confidence in the church's formal procedures is declining. Neither the remaining minority nor the regnant majority has much interest in the general assembly and its institutions. The years of pitched battle have

---

14 Hart, *Defending the Faith*, 153.
15 Ibid., 157.
16 Ibid.

ended, replaced by days of indifference. Synods are invisible. The system of judicial commissions is distrusted. Too many presbyteries are viewed as duties to be endured rather than councils of communion and discernment. The general assembly is ignored whenever possible, hoping that it will do no harm or, at least, not cause embarrassment.

Polity dies, not by its dismantling, but by the decline of its significance in the life of the faithful. More is at stake than the weakening of the polity's instruments. Polity is the articulation of the shape of common life, so that when polity dies common life deteriorates. Congregations and their pastors look to their own fidelity and well-being, unconcerned with the whole. Presbyteries look inward to their financial, staff, and missional woes. General Assembly actions and programs are ignored. Can the dry bones of polity live? God knows, but we are not consigned to passive waiting. The church is called to abandon endless rounds of organizational revision, as if different rules and configurations can restore ecclesial health. The church is called to think theologically about the shape of its life together in a renewed spirit of mutual tolerance and institutional forbearance.

Presbyterian *Episkopē* and the Good of the Church
Mutual tolerance and institutional forbearance, guardrails so necessary to the proper functioning of Presbyterian polity, will not be reinstated by resolutions encouraging or requiring them. It will take more than critique of their absence and urging their renewal to bring about a return to 'life together'. The starting point is renewed attention to what polity itself is intended to accomplish. Recovery of the purposes of *episkopē* – oversight – especially the *episkopē* exercised by presbyteries, may be key, leading to reform of sessions on the one hand, and the general assembly on the other.

Help in this task may come from an unexpected source: The World Council of Churches (WCC). The WCC's Faith and Order Commission has spent almost two decades working on drafts of a 'convergence document', *The Church*, intended to provide Orthodox, Catholic, Protestant, and Pentecostal Churches with a shared understanding of the nature and purpose of the church. The draft document includes an ecumenically recognizable description of *episkopē*. It begins by setting out three foundational responsibilities of *episkopē*, whether exercised by bishops or by councils such as presbyteries:

> (…) *episcopé* is in the service of maintaining continuity in apostolic faith and unity of life. In addition to preaching the Word and celebrating the

Sacraments, a principal purpose of this ministry is faithfully to safeguard and hand on revealed truth, to hold the local congregations in communion, to give mutual support and to lead in witnessing to the Gospel.[17]

Episkopē is not a free-standing ecclesial reality, however. Faith and Order's useful description, centered on maintenance of apostolic faith, unity of life, and witnessing to the gospel can only be understood fully by working backward from its source. *Episkopē* begins, not with the church, but with the Lord of the church. The church is not its own; the church is always *creatura verbi* – the body of Christ, the people of God, the communion of the Holy Spirit. When *episkopē* is narrowly conceived as the church's own work of preserving the ancient 'deposit of faith', maintaining (remnants of) the originating gift of unity, and calling whatever it does 'mission', it is little more than a bureaucratic mechanism of institutional control.

Calvin noted that the governance of the church always originates in Christ, 'For [the church] has Christ as its sole Head, under whose sway all of us cleave to one another, according to that order and that form of polity which he has laid down'.[18] Imagine the shape of our conciliar life if our 'form of polity' in presbyteries were shaped by coming together in prayer and study to exercise our continuous responsibility to discern the shape of apostolic faith, hold congregations together in deep communion, and lead and support congregations in bearing witness to the gospel in word and action.

Continuity in Apostolic Faith

What is meant by 'apostolic faith'? A World Council of Churches Faith and Order project set out a kinetic rather than static understanding: 'The term *apostolic faith* (…) does not refer to a single fixed formula, nor to a specific moment in Christian history. Rather, it points to the dynamic reality of the Christian faith'. This dynamic reality is understood as expressing the trajectory from Scripture's apostolic witness through the foundational Nicene-Constantinopolitan Creed and the ecumenical creeds that followed from it, to historic and contemporary explications of that trajectory 'in confession, in preaching, in worship and in the Sacraments of the Church as well as in creedal statements, decisions of councils and confessional texts, and in the life of the church'.[19]

---

17 *The Church,* III.A.52, 29.
18 Calvin, *Institutes,* IV.VI.9, 1110.
19 *Confessing the One Faith,* Faith and Order Paper n°. 153, 2f.

The reception, preservation, contextualization, transmission, and incorporation of apostolic faith has always been a complex process. Current American cultural reality further complicates the complexity. The ascendance of procedure and the marginalization of theological norms in many North American churches is reinforced by cultural assumptions of individual self-determination. Theological and moral claims are met by widespread distrust of 'oppressive orthodoxy', coupled with the pervasive conviction that diversity is the desired theological norm. Only procedure is 'fair to all'. The result is that maintaining continuity in apostolic faith has become marginal to the churches' practice of *episkopē*. Church councils meet and make numerous decisions that affect ecclesial life, but their decision-making is based on cultural, legal, economic, pragmatic, and procedural grounds rather than on articulations of the church's faith.

Ensuring continuity in apostolic faith is an essential element of *episkopē*, yet the conciliar practice of churches is susceptible to erring by omission. Because vaguely shared faith is simply assumed, explicit norms of apostolic faith and life play only a minor role in councils' ongoing exercise of ecclesial oversight. The responsibility of councils 'faithfully to safeguard and hand on revealed truth (…) and to lead in witnessing to the Gospel' is not rejected, but it is most often marginalized or neglected in practice and is rarely at the center of councils' self-understanding.

Maintaining continuity in apostolic faith begins with honest assessment of the church's life in congregations, presbyteries, and the general assembly. Every form of denominational *episkopē* is called to 'self-interrogation', asking whether its *form* is actually *exercised* 'in the light of the Christological, pneumatological and ecclesiological principles of the gospel'. Such self-interrogation is not answered by abstract reference to confessional standards, official polity, or formal statements, but by renewed attention to the gospel 'which we received, in which we stand, by which we are saved, if we hold it fast' (cf. 1 Cor 15:1-2).

Unity of Life
Maintaining unity of life among congregations and judicatories is a primary responsibility of *episkopē*. It is also a pragmatic institutional aim, necessary for organizational maintenance. But the absence of serious sustained attention to continuity in apostolic faith reduces church unity to mere institutional connection. Assumed unity, dependent on church law, bureaucratic organization, parliamentary procedure, and majority vote decision-making has often become a recipe for disunity of both life

and institution. Democratic legislative procedures have been instituted and employed by churches for good and faithful reasons; they open matters of faith and life to the whole membership of the church. However, in our time, the capacity of conciliar *episkopē* to fulfill its most fundamental purposes is weakened by its captivity to proceduralism. James Davison Hunter contends that developments in American political culture have produced 'a tendency toward the politicization of nearly everything'. Including church councils. 'Politicization', says Hunter, 'is the turn toward law and politics – the instrumentality of the state – to find solutions to public problems'. The result (supplementing Hunter) is that 'the language (and practice) of politics comes to frame progressively more and more of our understanding of our common (ecclesial) life, our (ecclesial) purposes, and of ourselves individually and (ecclesially)'.[20]

Paul's use of the rich word *koinōnia* suggests a different possibility. It is variously rendered in English translations as *communion, fellowship, participation, partnership, sharing, contribution,* and *taking part*. Thus, readers who are confined to translations of the New Testament are unaware that one Greek word underlies disparate English vocabulary. This, in turn, prevents readers from noticing scriptural relationships among such seemingly dissimilar matters as lived communion with the Triune God; communion in faith, hope, and love; communion in sacraments; communion in the truth of the gospel; communion in faithful living; communion in the reconciliation of differences; and communion in patterns of mutual responsibility and accountability.

The unified vision of *koinōnia* in the life of the church may be illustrated through its entrance into English by way of its Latin equivalent, *communio*. Oliver O'Donovan notes the ways in which English nouns render *communio* in everyday speech:

> concrete 'community' on the one hand, dynamic 'communion' or 'communication' on the other. To communicate, to commune, says O'Donovan, is to hold some thing as common, to make it a common possession, to treat it as 'ours' rather than 'yours' or 'mine'. The partners to a communication form a community, a 'we' in relation to the object in which they participate.[21]

'We-ness' is at the heart of *koinōnia* – overcoming distance, ending partition, ceasing detachment, dwelling in mutuality – all in faith, hope, and love of God through Christ in the Spirit.

---

20 Hunter, *To Change the World*, 102f.
21 O'Donovan, *The Ways of Judgment*, 242.

It is 'we-ness', spoken and enacted relationships within and among congregations, denominations, and global families of churches that is *koinōnia's* substance and aim. The congregation is a *communion* of persons, born in the waters of baptism and nurtured at the Eucharistic table. Each congregational communion of persons is called to ecclesial communion with other congregations in its presbytery. Presbytery communions are called to broader patterns of denominational communion that lead toward ecumenical communion in the church catholic. In every instance, genuine communion is more than a pattern of institutional arrangements, for *koinōnia's* actuality is found in deep, intimate, abiding mutuality that has its source in the limitless grace of the Lord Jesus Christ, the overflowing love of God, and the all-embracing communion of the Holy Spirit.

The central task of presbyteries could shift from maintaining structural relationships to developing and maintaining communion – 'we-ness' – among pastors, among sessions, among congregations. Unity of life is not found in structural allegiance, but through participation in a 'we' that is grounded in the continuity of apostolic faith.

Bearing Witness to the Gospel
How is the church to proclaim the gospel in a secular age? The answer begins with a negation. The church is called to turn away from its characteristic proclamation of itself – marketing its attractive suite of religious goods and services – and turn toward God's new Way in the world in and through Jesus Christ, crucified risen and ascended. But how is this to be done in an age when fewer people are interested in what the church has to say? Even a strengthened, clarified, unified proclamation of the gospel is easily muffled by the cacophony of conflicting messages proclaiming alternate 'salvations', from hedonism and self-improvement to narcissistic mysticism, from expanding rights and genetic engineering to saving the planet. Even at its best, the church is but one voice in a world inundated with words. In an age when religious faith in general, and Christian faith in particular, is but one option among many, how is the gospel to be heard, and how will hearing lead to faith?

Bearing witness to the gospel requires clarity about the shape of the gospel and communal engagement in living the gospel. Thus, the exercise of *episkopē* in fostering continuity in apostolic faith and unity of life is essential to its responsibility to lead the church in bearing witness to the gospel. Presbyteries bear a particular obligation to ensure that pastors and congregations exercise the spiritual disciplines that undergird loving

God with heart, soul, mind, and strength, and loving neighbors beyond the church, both near at hand and far afield. *For what we preach is not ourselves, but Jesus Christ as Lord* (2 Cor 4:5).

Reconstructing Guardrails
Continuity in apostolic faith, unity of life, and witness to the gospel are not programmatic initiatives generating competing goals, strategies, and tactics, leading to proposals that are submitted to votes. They are the ongoing responsibilities of *episkopē*. The church's councils – sessions, presbyteries, synods, and the general assembly – can be liberated from captivity to the strictures of parliamentary procedure, set free for *koinōnia* in the grace of the Lord Jesus Christ, the love of God, and the communion of the Holy Spirit. Repair of the organizational guardrails of mutual tolerance and institutional forbearance is not the prerequisite, however. Serious, sustained attention to the faith, centered on Scripture, prayer, focused theological work, and sacraments will generate a quality of faithful life together in which mutuality and forbearance are once again as natural as breathing.

This is more than wishful thinking. Michael Jinkins' provocatively titled book, *The Church Faces Death*, points to the possibilities inherent in polity's terminal illness. Utilizing insights from psychological realities of human death and dying, Jinkins articulates an ecclesial parallel:

> When the church faces the prospect of its own demise, (…) it faces a critical moment when its vocation is called into question, when it has the unparalleled opportunity to comprehend and to render its life. When the church faces death (…). it encounters a critical moment when it may know the power of resurrection. But the church can only know this power in actually facing its death.[22]

If the Presbyterian Church can face the prospect of polity's demise, it can call its practice of *episkopē* into question. This could become an unparalleled opportunity to understand and assess its life as a community of Christian faith and faithfulness. If the church faces polity's death honestly it can encounter new possibilities of *episkopē*. But the church can only know this possibility if it actually faces the death of its polity.

---

22 Jinkins, *The Church Faces Death*, 13f.

Bibliography

Confessing the One Faith, Faith and Order Paper nº. 153. Geneva: WCC Publications, 1991.

Hart. D.G. *Defending the Faith: J. Gresham Machen and the Crisis of Conservative Protestantism in Modern America*. Phillipsburg NJ, 1994.

Hunter, James Davison. *To Change the World: The Irony, Tragedy, and Possibility of Christianity in the Late Modern World*. New York: Oxford University Press, 2010.

Jinkins, Michael. *The Church Faces Death*. New York: Oxford University Press, 1999.

Levitsky, Steven, and Daniel Ziblatt. *How Democracies Die*. New York: Crown, 2018.

Machen. J. Gresham. *Christianity and Liberalism*. Grand Rapids: Eerdmans, 1923.

Marsden. George M. *Fundamentalism and American Culture: The Shaping of Twentieth Century Evangelicalism 1870-1925*. New York: Oxford University Press, 1980.

O'Donovan, Oliver. *The Ways of Judgment*. Grand Rapids MI: Eerdmans, 2005.

Small. Joseph D. "The Democratic Captivity of the Church." In *Protestant Church Polity in Changing Contexts I: Ecclesiological and Historical Contributions*. Allan Janssen and Leo Koffeman, eds. Zürich: LIT Verlag, 2014, 49–63.

Small, Joseph D. "Presbyterianism's Democratic Captivity." *First Things*, nº. 221, March, 2012.

Snow. C.P. *The Two Cultures and a Second Look*. 2nd ed. Cambridge: The University Press, 1964.

Presbytery as the Engine of the Church

John P. Chalmers

Introduction

Church structures and polities grow out of historical circumstances and often these structures and polities owe as much of their origin to the wishes of a king, the relationship between church and state or the state of a relationship between two nations, as they owe to doctrinal standards or confessions of faith. In Scotland we like to believe that the driving force for our Presbyterian polity was our doctrinal understanding, but the truth is much more complex. This brief contribution shares a little of the complex history of the emergence of Presbyterian government as the dominant force in Scottish religious life, but it also seeks to explore ways in which the classis or the presbytery itself might recover some of its original potency and, in particular, its role as a *bishop* in the church.

When Martin Luther, the father of the sixteenth-century Protestant reformation in Europe, pinned his ninety-five theses to the door of the church in Wittenberg, no one could have predicted the far reach that his radical ideas and distinctive theology would have. That was 31 October 1517; it was ten years later that Patrick Hamilton, the brilliant son of Sir Patrick Hamilton and Catherine Stewart, (who was granddaughter of James II of Scotland) brought the radical doctrines of Luther to the shores of Scotland.

Patrick Hamilton had gone to study at the University of Paris where he came under the influence of Luther's writings; this in turn led him to Leuven to engage with the thinking of Erasmus. He was smitten and when he came back to Scotland in 1527 he chose St. Andrews – the great center of church and of learning – to preach this new free Gospel of justification by faith alone and of the priesthood of all believers. Hamilton's teachings were brought to the attention of James Beaton the Archbishop of St. Andrews, who ordered Hamilton to be arrested and formally tried for heresy.

He was condemned as a heretic and on February 29th 1528 he was burnt at the stake outside the front entrance to St. Salvator's Chapel in St. Andrews. Patrick Hamilton was, in fact, almost alone as a player on the

Scottish stage at this point in the early years of the reformation in Europe; but, his story and the brutal act of his execution, as much as anything else made Scotland fertile ground for fundamental change in the life of the church and the nation. Nothing drew so much attention to his teachings as his martyr's death – so much so that it was said that if others were to be treated in like fashion the burning should be done in cellars, 'for the reek of Master Patrick Hamilton had infected as many as it blew upon'.

The patrons of the Catholic Church, however, did not see the folly of suppressing this new expression of religion in this way. Movements are strengthened by martyrs' blood, so the sixteenth-century protestant reformation spread with relentless energy, Tyndale's translation of the New Testament was smuggled across from Holland, the Scottish Parliament in 1543 made lawful the reading of the Bible in the vulgar tongue, and the abuses of the Catholic Church continued. The latter received public, high profile and damning criticism in popular pamphlets which poured off the printing presses – the mass media channel of the day.

Upon this scene arrived the religious reformer George Wishart who popularised the teachings of Calvin and Zwingli. His career led him into a collision course with Cardinal David Beaton and he suffered the same fate in the same town that had overtaken Patrick Hamilton eighteen years earlier. At his trial he refused to accept that confession was a sacrament, denied free will, reiterated the priesthood of all believers, and rejected the idea that the infinite God could be 'comprehended in one place' between 'the priest's hands'. He proclaimed that the true church was where the Word of God was faithfully preached and the two dominical sacraments (Baptism and Holy Communion) were rightly administered. His death led, just a few months later, to the bloody murder of Cardinal Beaton and the whole of religious Scotland was plunged into holy war.

George Wishart's real legacy, however, was in the fact that John Knox was one of his disciples and followers. It was Wishart's mind and Wishart's blood that brought John Knox to the forefront of the Scottish Reformation. In the wake of Beaton's murder Knox fled Scotland and was thus brought into contact with John Calvin – it was from this source that he brought back to Scotland the distinctive insights into doctrine, worship, government and discipline which Calvin had devised for the church organised by him in Geneva.

If we are to understand the DNA of Presbyterianism it is in the precepts that Knox brought back to Scotland:

- a rejection of the apostolic tradition and an affirmation of the supremacy of scripture
- worship stripped of ceremony and ritual
- church government without a hierarchy of individuals
- instead an ascending series of courts – local, regional and national
- a church – autonomous in matters of doctrine, worship, government and discipline, and
- a church overseen by courts, populated by ministers and elders none of whom had any status above the others (a priesthood of all believers) – even the very terms clergy and laity would be rejected.

By 1560 the Scottish Reformation was secure. In 1559 the Latin Mass had been officially abolished by the Scottish Parliament and in 1560 the Scots Confession and the First Book of Discipline dealing with doctrine and government received the approval of Parliament. At this time membership of the nation and membership of the church were practically co-terminus; the only thing left to settle was the durability of Presbyterianism over Episcopacy as a form of government for the Scottish Church.

History records that, save for brief and hostile periods at the end of the sixteenth century and then again in the seventeenth century when episcopacy was thrust on the Scottish people (by the Stewart Kings), Presbyterian polity has been consistently maintained by the church and the nation:

- Since 1690 Presbyterianism has been recognised by the Crown. Its maintenance was ratified by Act of Security, in 1707 in the Treaty of Union.
- Ever since that time the signing of the Oath of Security for the Church of Scotland in its Presbyterian polity has formed the first duty of the Sovereign on ascension to the throne of Great Britain.
- Year on year in a letter sent to the General Assembly of the Church of Scotland, the Monarch renews the pledge – 'to preserve and uphold the rights and privileges of the Church of Scotland'.
- This is code that *episkopē* will not be forced upon the nation of Scotland and that Presbyterian government will be maintained.

Essentially, it was the aim of the Reformers to recall the simplicity and equality which they believed were characteristic of the early church. In this they believed that the New Testament image of the presbyter and the bishop were identical; the distinction being one of qualification and function rather than that of rank or authority. The underlying principle was one of parity among the ordained and that parity reaching beyond the role and function of the Ordained Minister of Word and Sacrament to embrace also the Ordained Elder.

One definition of Presbyterianism would be to say that it is government by spiritual leaders where the spiritual leaders are those who have been ordained as teaching elders (Ministers of Word and Sacrament) and ruling elders (those who in Kirk Session are responsible for local church management, spiritual oversight and pastoral care) and now Deacons (those who are ordained to a servant ministry). No *one* spiritual office is superior to another, they are just different in function. The so called, 'highest Office' would be that of the Moderator of the General Assembly; an office which can be held by any one of the ordained spiritual leaders. But even while she or he holds that office for the one year for which she or he is elected – she or he is thereby raised to no higher a rank. For the time that person holds office they are *primus inter pares* – first [only] among equals.

In Presbyterian polity the idea of parity in ministry is so strong that, in spite of obvious differences, it is held that there is no distinction in status between those who are ordained to office (whether to the Ministry of Word and Sacrament, the Diaconate or the Eldership) and those who belong to what might be termed the *ordinary* membership of the church. This derives from that great pillar of the Protestant Reformation – the doctrine of the priesthood of all believers. The evangelical calling of the church was no longer to be the domain of the clergy alone; instead each individual member of the body of Christ was to understand their calling as a part of the ministry of Jesus Christ exercised through the *whole people of God*. The proof text of this was an understanding of 1 Peter 2:9, "But you are not like that, for you are a chosen people. You are royal priests, a holy nation, God's very own possession. As a result, you can show others the goodness of God, for he called you out of the darkness into his wonderful light."

Another definition of Presbyterianism is to say that it is government by courts. It is certainly an embedded principle that Presbyterian government is conciliar in polity. The Presbytery and not its moderator is the bishop. The General Assembly and not its moderator is the archbishop. The only real hierarchy within Presbyterianism is the hierarchy of its courts.

But, one of the most interesting facts is that in its original conception Presbyterianism was a three-tier system. The Kirk Session stood at the base of the triangle, the general assembly was its apex and it was the provincial synod (not the presbytery) which was sandwiched between the two. So, we discover that Presbyterian polity in Scotland was first established without presbyteries.

The provincial synod as the name suggests was the court of regional affairs, but in days when large regional gatherings were difficult to arrange and time consuming to manage – smaller, more informal local gatherings for study, prayer and spiritual exercise were arranged. From these more local meetings the presbytery was formed and you can imagine why, at that time, we might have called it *the engine of the church;* for here, men (and at that time it was all men) were met to discern what Scripture might be saying to them in the context of the social upheaval and turmoil of their day, here men were met to pray, to invoke the power of the Holy Spirit, to study holiness and make themselves fit for purpose.

In other words, in its earliest conception the function of presbytery was deeply spiritual. When these men met, their business then was *not* business as we describe it now. Their business, instead, was 'to seek first the Kingdom of heaven' (Matthew 6:33) and it could be argued that we have paid a high price for the way in which that element of the life of our presbyteries has been allowed to be overtaken by legal, bureaucratic, disciplinary and ceremonial functions. And by an avalanche of responsibilities sent down by General Assemblies or raised up by Kirk Sessions.

That was Then, This is Now
If I am right, and Europe is no different from Scotland, then urgent change is needed in almost every part of the life our church. The structure of our version of Presbyterianism is groaning under the weight of too much bureaucracy. Presbyteries are groaning under the weight of too much administration and routine management and they have so much formal business to transact that they are being distracted from the urgent business of re-visioning the church.

All, however, is not despair. Presbyteries can once again be the engine of the church, but for that to happen presbytery reform is a crucial requirement and a large part of that must be the recovery of the presbytery as a place of spiritual nourishment and supportive fellowship.

Taking the Church of Scotland as an example it is possible to trace elements of presbytery life and culture which was and is:

- more often competitive than supportive
- more often concerned with discipline than with compassion
- more often driven by law than grace
- more focussed on *getting through the business* than on *stopping to pray*

In this section I offer some thoughts under these four bulleted headings and I do so searching for the kind of change that might make the life of our presbyteries more positive and more productive.

More often competitive than supportive

My own earliest memories of Presbytery meetings are of superintendence reports that left little doubt as to whether a congregation was succeeding or failing. Many were left feeling quite inadequate because other congregations seemed to be doing so much better than their congregation. It was like being in a league – some congregations were regarded as being in the Premiership, others were in the second division while others were struggling to avoid relegation and not being given much support or encouragement to grow and succeed.

More often concerned with discipline than with compassion

Another early memory of presbytery is of a full attendance of presbyters, because we were dealing with a matter of discipline. This was a minister on trial for some misdemeanour; this appealed to everyone's voyeuristic instinct. Such disciplinary meetings might last until well after mid-night with presbytery sitting as a court, examining, cross-examining, determining a verdict and imposing a sentence. In short, determining whether a career should come to an end because of some infraction of the rules or the holding of some doctrine considered to be heretical. Of course, matters of church discipline are of great importance, but nothing can excuse the damage done when these actions are bungled by amateurs. Happily much has been done in recent years to improve the way in which church discipline is managed in the Church of Scotland, but there is a sad chapter of our history which has contributed in large measure to a decline in the understanding of presbytery as a place where one could rely on finding support and fellowship.

More often driven by law than grace

There is another recurring weakness in Presbyterian polity and that is the ability we have of making matters of procedure seem more important that matters of substance. So, for instance, if you wanted to discuss a matter of great significance such as the place of children at the Communion Table – only a few presbyters will have anything to say about the theological implications of this matter but, there will be no end to the 'points of order' or 'procedural niceties' of how the debate should be conducted, the order in which the motions should be heard and the procedure for holding the vote.

More focussed on *getting through the business* than on *stopping to pray*
I well remember one presbytery meeting when the Moderator welcomed new members to the meeting with the words: "To those of you who are attending your first meeting of this presbytery, I hope that your lives are not so dull that you might consider this as being a good night out."

The inference was clear – we're not here to do anything terribly important and the sooner we can get through the agenda, then the sooner we can all get back home to watch the football or get on with more interesting things.

The reflections under each of these headings may not amount to much in themselves, but they serve to illustrate how far we have come from a time when our Presbyteries were organised to cater for the spiritual well-being of their members. It follows therefore, that if presbytery as a classis is once again to be the *engine of the church*, then under each of these headings there has to be a world of change.

More often competitive than supportive
We need to be reminded that we have a collective responsibility to one another. We are a priesthood of all believers accountable to one another. No one member of the presbytery is more important than the other, no one member able to survive on their own. If I had a bishop, I would expect my bishop to be at least as interested (if not more interested) in the weakest of the company as she or he might be interested in the strongest. *Presbytery is my bishop* and it has to learn how to share its resources, how to support the weakest and how to help the strongest remain humble.

More often concerned with discipline than with compassion
We wouldn't be Presbyterians if we didn't believe that everything should be done decently and in order. We would be forgetting our heritage if we did not acknowledge that discipline was an important function. The Scots Confession may have come first, but it was closely followed by the First Book of Discipline. However, it is easy to discern that we became somewhat obsessed with policing the morality of the flock and for too long we have allowed an over-bearing Calvinist ethic to dominate our life. In eighteenth century Scotland our national poet, Robert Burns, parodied that theology in some remarkable poems. The Address to The Unco Guid is a perfect example:

O ye wha are sae guid yoursel',
Sae pious and sae holy,
Ye've nought to do but mark and tell
Your neibours' fauts and folly!

In translation this refers to the pious *who think much of themselves,* who spend most of their time *pointing out the faults and failures of others;* while seeing none of their own shortcomings. This could be a translation of Matthew 7:5 referring to those who see the speck in another's eye while ignoring the log in their own.

We used to make those whom we judged to be sinners sit in disgrace on a penance stool (the Cutty Stool) in front of the congregation. One presbytery even banned the wearing of hats when sitting on the 'cutty stool' because the sinner had to be humiliated in full view. A church does not quickly recover from that kind of graceless hypocrisy and it is a long journey from that place to one where restorative justice, that focuses on the needs of the offended as well as the offender, becomes the order of the day.

If I had a bishop I would expect her or him to be as compassionate about my welfare as they were concerned about my moral propriety. The *presbytery is my bishop,* but, until now it has been better at judgement than it is at mercy and that needs to change.

More often driven by law than grace
We have to ask - when did Luther's clarion call, *by grace alone,* become saturated in practice and procedure and law and order?

An oft quoted and interesting digest of the development of Christianity says,

> In the beginning the church was a fellowship of men and women centring on the living Christ. Then the church moved to Greece, where it became a philosophy. Then it moved to Rome, where it became an institution. Next it moved to Europe where it became a culture, and, finally, it moved to America where it became an enterprise.

Of course, that is not a detailed mapping of the history of the church, but it is impossible to resist the reality that the narrative of our faith has strayed a long way from its roots in a community bound together by its love for Jesus of Nazareth.

If I had a bishop I would expect her or him to ask *how was my relationship with God* as regularly they asked me about how I spent my time in active service. *The presbytery is my bishop,* but it falls short in designing its life around ways of helping me to deepen my relationship with God or encouraging the kind of pastoral support which might help me and my fellow members hold fast to the faith against today's secular onslaught.

More focussed on *getting through the business* than on *stopping to pray*
In 2018, the General Assembly of the Church of Scotland sent down 78 instructions or discussion topics to its presbyteries, Kirk Sessions and congregations. If any one of those bodies made it their business to examine and discuss every one of those then they would do nothing else in the course of the year.

Now that would be fine, if those injunctions were focussed on enabling the mission and growth of the local church. But, while many of them are laudable in their own right they are so prolific that few people take them seriously and important stuff is lost in the storm of words. The structure, however, as we operate it demands that we go through the motions, tick the boxes, complete the marathon of words and it leaves us next to no time to reflect and study and pray. *The Word was made flesh and dwelt among us* (...) and we Presbyterians turned it back into words, words and more words.

If I had a bishop I would expect her or him to help me focus as much on the inner life as on the outer life. If I had a bishop I would expect her or him to reduce the number of goals set for me and my congregation to those that were manageable, measurable, realistic and achievable. *The presbytery is my Bishop,* but it has not learned for itself to set goals that are manageable, measurable, realistic and achievable.

So, as I contemplate the future of the church that has meant so much to me, I look back with some regret, that too much of my own time has been spent arguing over the philosophy, reorganising the institution, fretting about the membership and devising better ways of promoting the enterprise. This has mostly been at the expense of developing that relationship with Christ and at the expense of properly coming to terms with the transformation of life and of our understanding of God which is the far-reaching message of Jesus' ministry. It is a time, therefore, to recalibrate and spend less time on the peripheral stuff and more time on the relational stuff. This is what presbyters were doing in the 16th century when they first met for weekly spiritual exercises.

What Next
There are a number of essentials which have to be tackled if presbyteries are once again to be the engine of church and, high on the list of essentials must be the way in which they encourage cutting edge theological thinking and deep relationship with God and with one another.

It may sound odd to quote a Franciscan Friar in the context of a discussion on the classis or presbytery but Richard Rohr, that deeply insightful Franciscan has said, "Much of common religion today is ideology more than any real encounter with Presence, but abstract theology will not get you very far. When religion becomes mere ideology or theology, it starts – and stays – with universal theories and the rubber never hits the road."

The real truth today is that at the intersection of the church and real people, living on real streets, the *rubber is not hitting the road* and the traditional patterns of church life (with which I have been so comfortable) are not going to change that:

- A revolution in scientific understanding requires us to be able to speak of a God who is in and yet transcends all of life.
- People will not embrace old dogmas which may have been understandable in an age of less knowledge.
- Only a faith which speaks to the deepest needs of human life will be transformative for both individuals and the communities they belong to.

The most serious question of all question is this – are our presbyteries willing to be at the forefront of the change which is required in our church life? Because the purpose of God is not about saving denominations or institutions from extinction; the purpose of God and the mission of church is about building communities of justice and peace and love – our presbyteries can be a part of that mission or they can drift into irrelevance and obscurity.

Often Presbyterianism is visualised as a triangular in structure and most often this is shown with the General Assembly at the top of the triangle and the congregation or the Kirk Session at the bottom. This is true if you think of hierarchy, but it is not true if you think about what really matters in terms of what is the *front facing and most vital element of church*.

In 1999 the General Assembly of the Church of Scotland, seeking something of the mind and purpose of God for a new millennium, set up a Special Commission anent[1] Review and Reform. The Commission reported to the General Assembly in 2001, and they gave their report the title A Church Without Walls.[2] In particular, it described the Church of Scotland as having become too centralised and it called for the structures of the church to be turned upside down.

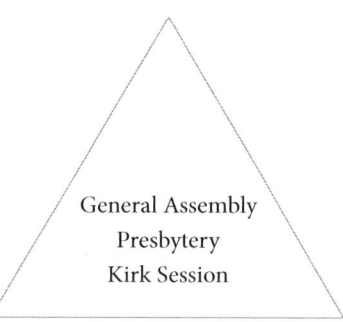

The triangle would therefore be inverted with the resources of people, of money, of buildings and of ministries all being channelled towards the strengthening and growing of local congregations.

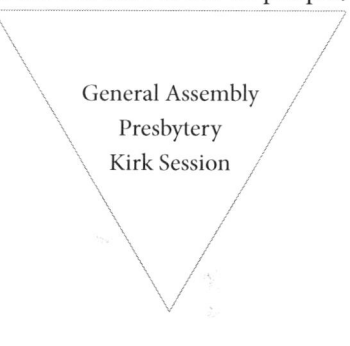

The same report described Presbyterianism, not as government by spiritual leaders and not as government by courts, but, instead it described Presbyterianism as having become a 'form of institutionalised distrust' and one can see where this comes from.

Between the General Assembly with all of its high level discussions and instructions and the congregations expected to carry these through, a great gulf has opened up. A blame culture has developed and a battle rages – between those who think that the church can be managed from the centre and those who have all but left the institution and are going it alone in a form of congregationalism.

---

1 ANENT – a Scottish word meaning, "*in relation to*".
2 http://www.churchofscotland.org.uk/__data/assets/pdf_file/0006/11787/CWW_REPORT_for_website_2Nov2012.pdf

It is interesting, that in 2015 for the first time the General Assembly of the Church of Scotland passed a measure[3] which, far from setting a national policy and practice in regard to the Ordination and Induction of Ministers and Deacons in Same Sex Relationships; it gave to individual congregations the right to decide for themselves whether they stood in the traditional or progressive camps of the church. There are many other examples of tensions that exist between the national and the local and many examples of disengagement, disconnection and disillusion between those who sit in the pew and those who occupy the central administration. My own view is that this will lead to ruin unless we recover the role of the presbytery.

Whichever version of the triangle is used – the pivotal and strategic position of the presbytery does not change. If Presbyteries are squeezed out of this sandwich what will save us from wholesale congregationalism? So, what presbyteries have to realise is that there is nothing more important than the filling in the sandwich. It's the filling that makes the sandwich. So, what might be in the filling that would cement the important position of presbyteries and once again make the presbytery into the engine of the church?

In the Scottish context, the Kirk Session and the congregation are at the frontline; they are the local face of the church, but in Scotland today 70 out of a 100 of our congregations do not have the resources they need to stand alone. In other words 30 out of a 100 congregations are paying their way (the costs of ministry, upkeep of buildings and local mission) and over and above that, they are providing the additional funds which go to subsidise the other 70.

This factor alone makes the regional body of the presbytery so significant to our future success. Honeybees in a beehive cannot survive as individuals they can only operate and succeed as a colony. It is the presbytery that can provide the wrap-around support of the colony. So that:

- no person has to work alone
- no minister is unsupported
- no one person has to be an expert in every discipline
- as well as being accountable to one another, people are responsible for one another

---

3 https://www.churchofscotland.org.uk/__data/assets/pdf_file/0004/27940/2015_Act_1_Ministers_and_Deacons_in_Civil_Partnerships_and_Same_Sex_Marriages.pdf

To achieve this we need to drop that element of competition. If you are familiar with the way in which military regiments work you will know that a soldier is not trained to fight the enemy in front, but she/he is trained to fight with the person beside them.

I am very glad that in Scotland we have removed the disciplinary function from the local court – this is now handled by a national commission. It leaves presbyters in a position where they will never have to stand in judgement of one another. They now need to use that space to build systems of pastoral support and peer appraisal.

While our presbyteries are a part of the legal structure of our church – we are not living in days when a legalistic approach to the challenges we face will do us any good. Once upon a time our Kirk Sessions were legalistic and disciplinarian – now the best Kirk Sessions are engaged in strategic thinking and missionary planning. That must be the role of our presbyteries.

The advantage that presbytery has is that it can pool talent and resources and implement initiatives that congregations left to their own devices could never put into operation. Let me give you one strong example.

The Church of Scotland last year opened its first online church[4] and it is offering a spiritual push to your mobile device every day. It is making available access to worship, prayer, Bible study and spiritual reflection that no single congregation could ever contemplate. It is a presbytery based initiative and it is challenging us to think about what it means to belong to the church. Can you be a member of a virtual community? How do you connect fast growing digitally based congregations with real people? Can you celebrate the Lord's Supper online or even baptise a child from an internet studio?

I don't know the answer to all of these questions, but I do know that the ways in which we understand Sabbath and the ways in which we help to sustain people on their spiritual journey and nourish their inner life in our 24/7 culture has to change; and I *want my bishop (the presbytery)* to be at the forefront of that work.

Finally, I want my bishop to be business driven, but that needs to be as much about the business of prayer as it is about the business of meeting real local needs and setting the bar for building communities of love and love for justice.

I am proud that my General Assembly deals with many and wide ranging issues. It is important for us to discuss our views on such things

---

4 http://www.sanctuaryfirst.org.uk

as the labelling of goods from Israeli settlements in the West Bank to expressing our view on the National Lottery; from the priority of the church to serve the poor in Scotland and beyond to our policy on education and training for the ministry; these are important matters for national debate and discussion. But *I want my bishop, the presbytery*, to filter all this stuff so that I am not duplicating what has already been done and I am freed to focus on the priorities which will contribute to the development and growth of the local church.

In Church of Scotland circles it is often said that Presbyterianism is the slowest of all the evolving organisms of life and that is why we do not respond with agility to our rapidly changing world and an illustrious predecessor of mine once said 'you can have Presbyterianism or you can have efficiency, but you cannot have both'.[5]

Perhaps this was only in jest or a lament on the glacial pace with which change in a Presbyterian system takes place. I think, however, that efficiency can be achieved, but it means that those bodies on either side of the presbytery have to realise their limitations and give presbyteries the resources and the space that only the regional platform can occupy. The best supercars have their power plants somewhere in the middle – they are described as mid-engine models. Presbyterianism already has a mid-engine structure, we just have to give that engine the fuel it needs and it could be the engine of change and the engine of the church.

Bibliography

Burleigh, J.H.S. *A Church History of Scotland*. Edinburgh: Hope Trust, 1960.

Burns, Robert. *Poems and Songs of Robert Burns*. London/Glasgow: Collins, 1955.

Cox, James T. *Practice and Procedure of the Church of Scotland*. 6th ed. [Edinburgh]: The Committee on General Administration, 1976.

Davies, J.G. "Priesthood of all Believers." *A Dictionary of Christian Theology*. ed. Alan Richardson. London: SCM Press Ltd, 1969.

---

5 Attributed to The Very Rev Dr James Weatherhead, former Moderator and former Principal Clerk to the General Assembly of the Church of Scotland.

Duke, John A. *History of the Church of Scotland to the Reformation.* Edinburgh/London: Oliver and Boyd, 1937.

Herron, Andrew. *Kirk by Divine Right.* Edinburgh: St Andrew Press, 1985.

Herron, Andrew. *The Law and Practice of the Kirk.* Glasgow: Chapter House, 1995.

McGrath, Alister E. *Christian Theology.* 5th ed. Chicester: Wiley-Blackwell, 2011.

Maclean, Marjory A. *The Crown Rights of the Redeemer.* Edinburgh: St Andrew Press, 2009.

Digital sources

https://www.barrypopik.com/index.php/new_york_city/entry/when_christianity_came_to_america_it_became_a_business

http://www.churchofscotland.org.uk/__data/assets/pdf_file/0006/11787/CWW_REPORT_for_website_2Nov2012.pdf

https://www.churchofscotland.org.uk/__data/assets/pdf_file/0004/27940/2015_Act_1_Ministers_and_Deacons_in_Civil_Partnerships_and_Same_Sex_Marriages.pdf

https://www.merriam-webster.com/dictionary/cutty%20stool

http://www.scotshistoryonline.co.uk/union.html

http://www.churchofscotland.org.uk/__data/assets/pdf_file/0004/48199/Supplementary_reports_2017_volume_3.pdf

http://www.sanctuaryfirst.org.uk

Rohr, Fr. Richard, 14 June 2017, https://cac.org/one-sacred-universe-2017-06-14/

Afterword

Allan J. Janssen

For the churches of the sixteenth-century protestant Reformation, the order of the church was not only a practical, but a theological matter. In rejecting the hierarchical system, with authority vested in the bishop on the one hand, and a congregational system on the other hand, the question presented itself: how is the church governed in obedience to the will of God? The (developed) answer was the synodical system. At the heart of that system was and is the 'middle judicatory' the classis or the presbytery.[1] A body that stood between the general synod (or assembly) and the local consistory (session, church council) was more local than the greater body; it consisted of 'neighboring churches' (Emden, VII), but drew local congregations into a greater body. Because these 'mediating' bodies were constituted by delegated office-bearers whose primary responsibilities were in service of the congregations, the classis has been a continuing issue. How are requisite governance tasks, some quite demanding, to be accomplished in collegial assemblies? Indeed, how do these modest bodies manifest those very *notae ecclesia* that are confessed as the attributes of the true church: unity, catholicity, holiness, and apostolicity? These have been, and continue to be, pressing issues for Reformed churches, not only as they strive to be faithful and obedience churches, but in the greater ecumenical dialogue. The history of the Reformed churches from the sixteenth century is evidence of the churches wrestling with the place and position of the classis in the life of the church.

The essays in this volume (as well as in its predecessor volume) on the one hand manifest the lively continuing interest in the nature and function of the classis and on the other hand bear witness to the pressure under which the classes function. I suspect that the pressure that is being felt has less to do with the classis as a structured body within the church than it has to do with anxiety about the nature and state of the church at the present time. This presents itself in a number of ways. The long march of secularization has removed the church from the center of society. That is coupled with a correspondingly long decline in church membership and

---

1 For the sake of brevity, references to the 'classis' include the presbytery.

attendance. The practical result is that fewer persons are available to share in the leadership of the church, and if leadership is available, in the person of ordained elders and deacons, in the local congregation, many of them have little interest or energy in participating in the sometimes time and energy consuming tasks of governance at a non-local level. In addition, certain societal changes have altered the landscape. Leon van den Broeke, in his essay in this volume, noted how the appearance of railroads altered how the churches could cooperate. New information technologies now mean that people need not travel to meet but can gather virtually. Moreover, communities form that are no longer geographically limited. All this puts pressure on how the church governs itself through that modest body, the classis.

These essays have reflected that tension as some have detailed the history of the development of the classis in various cultures. Others describe new attempts to enable the classis to function more appropriately. In the previous volume, my co-editor and colleague Leon van den Broeke portrayed a continuum between two functions that a classis is expected to fulfill, that of *episkopē* at the one pole and *koinōnia* at the other.[2] More and more classes have found themselves bogged down on the *episkopē* end of the spectrum and longed for a greater sense of fellowship. Classes had become too administrative.

Nonetheless, a deep aversion to the figure of a bishop remains among the Reformed churches. This is a resistance to authority consolidated in the hands of one person. This is even the case with the Protestant Church of the Netherlands with its new position of the 'classis minister' or 'half-bishop' in the words of Klaas-Willem de Jong. That church resisted the characterization of this figure as a 'bishop'.

Moreover, the churches evidence difficulty fulfilling the episcopal responsibilities of the classis. In part this is the result of an aversion by many to the task of governance itself. Not all office-bearers possess the requisite gifts for administrative decision-making or of disciplinary oversight. The time required to perform the necessary functions – and to do so in community! – is simply overwhelming. Coupled with that, and in part for those reasons, it has become more difficult to find office-bearers willing to participate in the governance of the church.

I noted above that alterations in regulations concerning the classis in church orders is also a function of reflection on the nature of the church. As some churches have understood themselves as *missional* in nature,

---

2 Van den Broeke, "The Protestant Classis: Between Episcopè and Koinonia," 75–92.

they have reshaped their church orders to reflect that reality. This has impacted how the church order sees the work of the classes. This, too, means the continuing evolvement of the nature of the classis itself.

Nonetheless, the classes will continue to exercise their episcopal functions. Ministerial oversight, supervision of the churches, care of ministerial candidates and responsibility for ordination of ministers of Word and Sacrament, disciplinary oversight of ministerial conduct, management of congregational conflicts, all need sustained care and attention. If it is not the classis that performs these responsibilities, then what body (or person) is there to do them?

So thus far the classes continue. We have yet to experience the results of newer experiments. We can only work together as we wait with hope for positive results. In the meantime, classes will continue to work, often with few resources other than the capability of office-bearers who understand the work as part of their ministry. And yet, the classis is close to the ground, much more so than the synods. Just so, the classes project the church both from bureaucratization on the one hand, and congregational isolation on the other.

The authors

The Very Rev **Dr John Chalmers** has served the church as Principal Clerk (2010 – 2017) and as Moderator (2014 – 2015) of the General Assembly of the Church of Scotland. Appointed as a Chaplain to the Queen in Scotland 2013 and for services to the church and wider society awarded an Honorary Doctor of Divinity degree from the Aberdeen University in 2016. Currently he serves the Church of Scotland as Convener of the Assembly Trustees and also Chairs the Carnegie UK Trust Action Group on access to affordable credit.

Adam Csukás is an internal doctoral student at the Department of Legal History of the Faculty of Law of Charles University in Prague. He works as a lawyer at the Central Church Office of the Evangelical Church of Czech Brethren.

Klaas-Willem de Jong is minister of the Protestantse Kerk in Nederland and Assistant Professor Church Polity at the Protestantse Theologische Universiteit (NL Amsterdam-Groningen). At this university he is also leader of the project 'The Dynamics of the Classical Reformed Liturgy in the Netherlands'

Dr. René de Reuver is pastor of the Protestant Church in The Netherlands. Since June 2016 he is the general-secretary of the General Synod of the Protestant Church in The Netherlands. Before he was a minister of the local congregations of Sebaldeburen (Groningen), Boskoop and The Hague. From 1987 until 2016 he was a member of three different classes. From 1999 until 2003 he represented the classis Alphen aan den Rijn in the General Synod. In 2005-2006 he was the chairman of this classis. From 2007-2015 he was the chairman of the General Council of Advice of the General Synod.

Allan J. Janssen (1948-2020) was Affiliate professor of Theological Studies emeritus, New Brunswick Theological Seminary. General Synod Professor emeritus, Reformed Church in America. He was the author of *Gathered at Albany: A History of a Classis* (1995) and *Constitutional Theology* (2001).

Joseph D. Small served as director of the Presbyterian Church (U.S.A.) Office of Theology and Worship from 1989-2011. He is now adjunct faculty at the University of Dubuque Theological Seminary and Pittsburgh Theological Seminary, and church relations consultant to the Presbyterian Foundation. He serves on the boards of the Center for Catholic and Evangelical Theology, the Institute for Church Renewal, and Innovative Space for Asian American Christianity.

Rev. Kathleen S. Smith is Senior Associate Director of the Calvin Institute of Christian Worship, Adjunct Professor of Church Polity at Calvin Theological Seminary, and Adjunct Professor of Congregational and Ministry Studies at Calvin University. Kathy is a graduate of Calvin College and Calvin Theological Seminary, an ordained minister in the Christian Reformed Church in North America, and the author of *Stilling the Storm: Worship and Congregational Leadership in Difficult Times* (Alban, 2006).

Leon van den Broeke is Associate professor Church Polity and Director of the Deddens Church Polity Centre at the Theologische Universiteit Kampen; Associate professor Religion, Law and Society and Chair of the Centre for Religion and Law at the Vrije Universiteit Amsterdam. He wrote a number of publications on the classis.

Index

Aberdeen University	139
Act of Security	121
Augsburg Confession, see Lutheran	87, 91
Austria, see Cisleithania (Austria) and also Austria-Hungary	85, 92, 96
Austria-Hungary	85, 92, 96
Baden, see also consistorialism	89
Battle of the White Mountain	86
Bavinck, Herman	28-29
Beaton, David	120
Beaton, James	119
Bednář, František	87
Beyer, Peter	44
bishop	3, 5, 15, 17, 23, 25, 29, 35, 37-38, 48, 55-59, 63-64, 67-68, 73, 82, 86-88, 95-98, 112, 119, 121-122, 125-127, 131-132, 135-136
board of elders, see also elders and local congregation	28, 32, 93
Bohemia, see Czech lands	91
Brethren, see Czech Brethren	5, 7, 24, 85-87, 91-95, 139
Burns, Robert	125
Calvin, John	29, 77, 113, 120
Calvin College	140
Calvin Theological Seminary	140
Čáslav Constitutional Movement, see Church Order of Čáslav	91
Catholic Church, see Roman Catholic Church	17, 28, 87, 96-98, 112, 120
Central Church Office	94
Chalmers, John	6, 22, 25, 119, 139
Charles University Prague	85, 139

church constitution	85, 87-89, 91-97
church council	15, 90-91, 93, 96, 114-115, 135
church order(s)	7, 16, 19, 21, 27-28, 30, 33, 35, 42, 48, 63-64, 68, 74-82, 89, 91-93, 96, 98, 104, 136-137
Church Order of Čáslav	91, 96
Church Order of Dort (DCO)	7, 30, 33, 77, 80, 91
church polity	2, 10, 12, 19, 21-22, 24-25, 42, 48, 85-86, 88-89, 91, 94-99, 139-140
Cisleithania (Austria)	89-92, 95-97
classical assembly passim	
classical committee(s)	25, 90, 94, 97-98
classical curators, see also *senior*	94
classis	96-97
classispredikant	5, 15, 23, 25, 38, 41-42, 48, 49, 55-56, 58, 60-68, 99
Comenius, John Amos	87
Communist dictatorship	93
congregational assemblies, see also local congregation	90
conseniores	95
consistorialism, see also Baden	89, 91
Csukás, Adam	5, 24-25, 85, 139
curator(s), see also classical curator and Synodical Curator	24, 89, 93-94, 98
Cyprian	29
Czech Brethren	5, 7, 24, 85, 92-94, 139
Czech lands	86-89
Czech Protestants	85-92, 95-97
Czech Reformation, see also Hus, Jan, Utraquist Church, Unity of the Brethren	85-87, 92, 95
Czech Republic	24, 26, 85, 92
Czechoslovakia	93
Daiber, Karl-Fritz	37
De Jong, Klaas-Willem	2, 5, 23, 48, 55, 136, 139
De Reuver, René	5, 15, 21, 139
De Vries, Jouke	47

denomination(s)	42, 46, 48-50, 59-60, 63, 66, 68, 73, 75, 78-81, 85-86, 91-94, 97-98, 108, 111
diaconate	122
Dijk, Gerrit van	8, 12
district(s)	43, 61, 90-91, 95-98
district assembly	91, 96
district committees	90
Dušek, Čeněk	95
ECCB, see Evangelical Church of Czech Brethren	7, 24-25, 85-86, 92-95, 97-99
elder(s), see also board of elders and local congregation	16, 18-19, 28, 30-33, 48, 64, 74-75, 78, 86, 89-90, 93, 97-98, 111, 121-122, 136
Enlightenment absolutism, see Patent of Toleration	87
episkopē	16, 21-24, 61, 67, 73, 76, 78-79, 112-117, 121, 136
episkopos	24, 89
Erasmus, Desiderus	119
Evangelical Church of Czech Brethren (ECCB)	5, 7, 24, 85, 92-94, 139
Evangelical Presbyterian Church	105
First World War	85, 92, 95
France	96
Francis Joseph, see Protestant Patent	89
General Assembly of Czech Protestants	92, 97
Glen Rock	9
Gosker, Margriet	57
Habsburg Empire, see also Cisleithania and Austria-Hungary	85, 88-89
Hamilton, Patrick	119-120
Hart, D.G.	111
Heartland	75

144 - Index

Helvetic Confession, see Reformed	87
hierarchy, see also kyriarchy	28, 31, 56, 60, 89, 96, 121-122, 128
Holland, Michigan	9
Houkes, Annemarie	43
Hungarian Lutheran Church	88
Hungarian Reformed Church	86, 88, 97
Hungary, see also Austria-Hungary	37, 85, 88, 92, 96, 106
Hunter, James Davison	115
Hus, Jan, see also Czech Reformation	86, 92
Hussite movement	86
Ignatius	29
Illiana	75
International Reformed Theological Institute (IRTI)	10-11
James II of Scotland	119
Janssen, Allan J.	3, 5-6, 9-12, 19, 21, 27, 37, 40, 135, 139
Jesus	15-17, 39, 49, 116-117, 122, 126-127
Jinkins, Michael	117
Joseph II, see Patent of Toleration	87
Kirk Session(s)	122-123, 127-131
Knox, John	120,
koinōnia	21-24, 38, 41, 61, 73, 76, 78-82, 115-117, 136
Kolle, Annemieke	43
Kronenburg, Hans	56-59, 67-68
Kuiper, Dick	43
kyriarchy, see also hierarchy	89
Leuven	119
Levitsky, Steven	106-107
local congregation(s)	15-18, 40, 49, 85, 90, 93-94, 113, 129, 135-136, 139
Lombard, Christo	10
Luther, Martin	119, 126
Lutheran(s)	20, 60, 87-92, 96, 98
Machen, J. Gresham	108-111
Marsden, George	105

Middle judicatory	23, 80, 135
minister(s)	15-19, 21, 23-24, 27, 30-31, 33-34, 38, 41, 46, 48, 55-57, 60-61, 63-64, 66, 68, 74-75, 81, 87-91, 93, 95, 97-98, 111, 121-122, 124, 130, 136-137, 139-140
Minnkota	75
Moravia, see Czech lands	87, 91, 95
Moravian Church, see Unity of the Brethren	87
Netherlands, the	5, 7, 10-11, 15, 19, 28, 37-39, 41, 43-47, 55-56, 60, 67, 85, 88, 99, 136, 139
New Brunswick Theological Seminary	9-10, 19, 37, 73, 139
Noordmans, Oepke	31
Oath of Security	121
O'Donovan, Oliver	115
Orthodox Presbyterian Church	105, 111
Paris	119
Patent of Toleration	87, 88, 95
Pella, Iowa	9
Pittsburgh Theological Seminary	140
Plaisier, Arjen	39
Port Ewen	9
presbyterial-synodical	16-18, 42, 48, 85, 98
Presbyterian Church (U.S.A.) (PCUSA)	7, 27, 32, 34, 103, 104, 108, 110, 111
Presbyterian church polity	24, 86, 88, 98
Presbyterianism	85, 91, 93, 96, 99, 103, 120-123, 128-129, 132
presbytery	3, 5-6, 10-11, 19, 21-23, 25-27, 37, 40, 56, 111, 116, 119, 122-132, 135
Protestant Church in Cisleithania (Austria)	89-92, 96-97
Protestant Church in the Netherlands/Protestantse Kerk in Nederland (PCN)	5, 7, 15, 17, 21, 23-25, 38-39, 41-42, 46-50, 55-56, 58-61, 63-68, 99, 139
Protestant Patent	89
Protestantism	85, 94

Protestantse Theologische Universiteit	10, 139
Reformatorisch Dagblad	8, 12
Reformed	5, 7, 9-12, 17-20, 22-23, 27-35, 37, 41, 56-57, 60, 63, 67, 73, 79, 86-92, 95-98, 135-136, 139-140
Reformed Church in America (RCA)	7, 9, 11-12, 28, 32-33, 139
Rhine-Westphalian Church Order	89, 98
Rohr, Richard	128
Roman Catholic Church, see Catholic Church	17, 87, 96
Rutte, Mark	46-47
Scheidemantel, Heinrich Gottfried	88
Schmitt, Carl	46
Scotland	25-26, 37, 63-64, 70, 85, 88, 91, 94, 96, 119-121, 123-125, 127, 129-132, 139
Scottish Reformation	120-121
Second World War	47, 93
Selkirk	9
senior(es), see also classical curator	25, 48, 94-96, 98-99
Shakespeare, Steven	41
Sheikh, Haroon	46
Simbolon, Lenta Enni	20
Slovak(ia)	24, 88-89, 98
Slovak Reformed Church	98
Small, Joseph D.	5, 22, 103, 140
Smith, Kathleen S.	2, 5, 22, 73, 140
Snow, C.P.	105
St. Andrews	119
St. Salvator's Chapel	119
Stated clerk(s)	80, 94, 110
Stewart, Catherine	119
synod(s)	9-10, 15-19, 21, 23-24, 27-30, 32-35, 37-42, 47-49, 55-57, 60, 63-65, 67, 73-75, 77-82, 88-91, 93-94, 97-98, 103-104, 112, 117, 122-123, 135, 137, 139

Synod of Emden	19, 30, 39, 47-49, 135
Synodical Committee	93, 95
Synodical Council(s)	93-94, 97-98
Synodical Curator	94
Synodical *Senior*	25, 94-95, 98-99
Theologische Universiteit Kampen	11, 19, 140
Treaty of Union	121
Trump, Donald	106
Tyndale	120
Unification	43, 92, 96
United Reformed Church (URC)	7, 23, 56, 63-68
United States of America (U.S.A.)	5, 19, 32, 34, 37, 73, 85, 91, 103-104, 140
Unity of the Brethren	86-87, 91, 94-95
University of Dubuque Theological Seminary	140
Utraquist Church	86-87
Vader, Albert	46
Van de Beek, Abraham (Bram)	10, 29, 31
Van den Broeke, C. (Leon)	2, 3, 5, 9, 19-20, 37, 56, 73-74, 136, 140
Van der Borght, E.A.J.G. (Eddy)	57, 67
Van Gelder, Craig	77, 80
Van Ruler, Arnold A.	10, 12
Vrije Universiteit Amsterdam	10-11, 140
Wainwright, Geoffrey	58
Weatherhead, James	132
Wishart, George	120
Wittenberg	119
Yellowstone	75
Ziblatt, Daniel	106-107
Zimmermann, Joseph Andreas	89
Zwingli, Hyldric	120